REFINED BY FIRE

STUDIES IN 1 & 2 PETER

J o h n   W .   S m i t h

ublished by 21st century christian

ISBN: 978-0-89098-542-7

eISBN: 978-0-89098-957-9

© Copyright by 21st Century Christian

2809 12th Ave S, Nashville, TN 37204

Cover Design by Jonathan Edelhuber

TABLE OF
CONTENTS

Introduction To First Peter 5

First Peter Chapter 1 7

First Peter Chapter 2 27

First Peter Chapter 3 43

First Peter Chapter 4 65

First Peter Chapter 5 83

Introduction To Second Peter 91

Second Peter Chapter 1 93

Second Peter Chapter 2 105

Second Peter Chapter 3 115

Notes On Calvin And Election 127

INTRODUCTION TO
FIRST PETER

The books of 1 and 2 Peter simply don't attract as much attention as, say, Ephesians, 1 Corinthians, and Romans. I'm sure there are several reasons for that. One of them may be that suffering is mentioned eighteen times in this book and it is one of the major themes. Talking about the benefits—even the desirability—of suffering won't attract much of an audience, especially in the United States where we avoid suffering at all costs and can certainly see no benefits in it. Peter was aware of the intense suffering that many Christians were undergoing for their faith (1 Peter 1:6; 3:14; 4:1, 12; 5:6, 10), and he was trying to encourage them.

I don't remember the first time I attempted to teach the book of 1 Peter, and I certainly don't remember the first time I read it. I'm sure it was more than fifty years ago. Whenever it was, it is remarkable that it made no lasting impression on me. Perhaps it was because I regarded the book as being rather simple and straightforward compared with the deep truths of Hebrews or Romans. It could also be that I regarded the rather impetuous, uneducated, simplistic writings of the fisherman as being somewhat inferior to the highly-educated, carefully-constructed doctrines and argumentation found in the writings of Paul.

Having taught the book numerous times and having discovered topics and ideas in it that have stretched me spiritually, I have developed a much greater appreciation for it. This adult study guide is the product of all of those years of class preparation and of the ideas and questions that have come to mind even in the very act of teaching. All of that wrestling with the expansive themes that are broached in this book has made me aware of why God has gone to the trouble of preserving it.

Some of the initial questions I think we ought to ask ourselves when we approach a book of the Bible is: "Why has God not only inspired this book, but what has He revealed in it that makes it uniquely important to the revelation of His will? What is found here that is found nowhere else in Scripture? Why has God gone to such great pains to see to it that it has been preserved over the centuries for us to read and learn from?"

One of the strange phenomena associated with writing a study guide like this is that the study guide always ends up being much longer than the book. But the Holy Spirit has always been able to say more in fewer words then man.

I have nothing to offer by way of historical background and setting for this book that cannot be found in any good study Bible. I do want to encourage those who might use this study guide to read the entire book before they begin their study and continue to do that periodically during the study. It is important to keep an overview of the scope of the entire book, which is easily lost as we go into lengthy investigation of particular principles and ideas contained in various verses.

FIRST PETER
CHAPTER 1

Peter, an apostle of Jesus Christ, To God's elect, strangers in the world, scattered throughout Pontus, Galatia, Cappadocia, Asia and Bithynia, who have been chosen according to the foreknowledge of God the Father, through the sanctifying work of the Spirit, for obedience to Jesus Christ and sprinkling by his blood: Grace and peace be yours in abundance (1 Peter 1:1, 2).

Peter begins his letter by affirming his apostleship and as a consequence, his ability to speak authoritatively on the matters to which he directs his attention. This would be of substantial importance to his readers as they quote his letter to others as a source of inspired instruction.

The book is written to Christians in the provinces of what is now northern and central Turkey, *possibly* from Rome (Babylon) in AD 63. In AD 64 Rome burned for six days, and Nero blamed the Christians and began his purge. The letter is addressed to "God's elect" (1 Peter 1:1) and to those who have been "chosen" by God for salvation.

The first sentence of the book introduces us to the somewhat nebulous doctrine of "election." In the 1600's the concept of election was seized upon, popularized, expanded upon and became the foundation of John Calvin's theology. Please refer to the section titled "Notes on Calvin and Election" located at the back of the book.

Peter refers to his audience as "strangers scattered in the world." Why "strangers" and why "scattered"? They were "strangers" because they had rejected materialistic values as the criteria for successful living. They were "scattered" because of persecution. These scattered Christians were predominantly Jews, but Gentiles were certainly included as is evidenced by 1 Peter 2:10 where Peter says, "Once you were not a people," which certainly refers to Gentiles.

Peter introduces us to three foundational but difficult doctrines in
1 Peter 1:1, 2: the doctrine of the Trinity; the doctrine of predestination
and election; and the work of the Holy Spirit in conversion.

A discussion of all of the implications surrounding the doctrine of
the Trinity is too consuming a project for this study, so the first idea I
want to pursue is the idea of *predestination.* The seemingly contradictory
ideas of free will and predestination have given students of the Word
problems for hundreds of years. The epistles are saturated with the
concept.

One of the most informative and inclusive passages on this topic is
found in Ephesians 1:4-14, where Paul writes

> For he chose us in him before the creation of the world to be holy
> and blameless in his sight. In love he predestined us to be adopted
> as his sons through Jesus Christ, in accordance with his pleasure and
> will—to the praise of his glorious grace, which he has freely given us
> in the One he loves. In him we have redemption through his blood,
> the forgiveness of sins, in accordance with the riches of God's grace
> that he lavished on us with all wisdom and understanding. And he
> made known to us the mystery of his will according to his good
> pleasure, which he purposed in Christ, to be put into effect when
> the times will have reached their fulfillment—to bring all things in
> heaven and on earth together under one head, even Christ. In him
> we were also chosen, having been predestined according to the plan
> of him who works out everything in conformity with the purpose of
> his will, in order that we, who were the first to hope in Christ, might
> be for the praise of his glory. And you also were included in Christ
> when you heard the word of truth, the gospel of your salvation.
> Having believed, you were marked in him with a seal, the promised
> Holy Spirit, who is a deposit guaranteeing our inheritance until the
> redemption of those who are God's possession—to the praise of
> his glory.

Paul says that God "chose us [Christians]" (Ephesians 1:4). What
does that mean? Remember that choosing does not at all imply that
there is no required response to the choice. God is not talking about
inanimate objects like blocks of wood or property. Choosing an object
is far different from choosing a person. Many a man who has chosen
a bride has learned that lesson well; she may not choose him. God's
choosing is for His purposes and it demands a response. Indeed, we must

in turn choose Him before God's purpose in election can be fulfilled. Our choosing is voluntary and requires an exercise of our will.

First Peter 1:22 says that we have purified ourselves by obeying the truth. That means that our purification was accomplished through our obedience; but obedience is an act of the will—not something imposed upon us. If our obedience to Christ is not a voluntary action, it is not to our credit and God can take no pleasure in it.

A careful reading of the Ephesians passage reveals the idea that God did not simply choose us in some general sense; rather He chose us to be something. First Peter 1:2 tells us that one of God's purposes in choosing us was "for obedience to Jesus Christ." Ephesians 1:4, 5 tells us two other purposes. First, He chose us that we would be "holy and blameless in his sight." Second, He chose us for adoption as "his sons." It is critical that we understand that all of God's choosing has to do with our being "in Christ." What does that mean? First, it means that God's choice for man's redemption is bound up exclusively in the advent, ministry, death, burial, and resurrection of Jesus. Second, it also means that God has not chosen anyone who is not in Jesus.

Paul goes on to say that, "[H]e predestined us to be adopted as his sons through Jesus Christ" (Ephesians 1:5). To predestine is a stronger concept than to choose, and its implications are even more unsettling. To predestine means to determine the outcome of events before they happen. Something predestined cannot be changed.

The question we might frame in this regard might be phrased like this: If God knew all these things (i.e., the fall, the cycle of rejection, rebellion, repentance, the history of sin), why in the name of anything that makes sense did He proceed? It is precisely the idea of what we mean by "makes sense" that causes us to stumble. "Makes sense" means that God's actions have to fit within the extremely limited confines of human reasoning. The only conclusive answer to our "why" question is that in God's infinite love, wisdom, justice, and mercy it was the best, wisest, and most loving thing to do. It suited His purposes.

What exactly did God predestine? Paul says "us"! Who is the "us"? "Us" is a collective pronoun referring first, specifically to the writer, Paul, and second to his audience—the congregation of believers at Ephesus—and third to all believers. What about "us" did God predestine? Notice that whatever He predestined for one believer, He predestined for all believers. It was not only the redeemed who were "destined." Peter writes in 1 Peter 2:8: "A stone that causes men to stumble and a rock that makes them fall." They stumble because they disobey the message—which is also what they were destined for. Peter says that the disobedient—the unbelievers—are also *destined* by God.

It is absolutely critical that we see that God's predestining was done as a result of His *love*—not arbitrariness, or as the result of divine whim or caprice. No concept of predestination that does not meet the criteria of God's unfathomable love and purpose of redemption is acceptable as an explanation. This is one of the great fallacies of Calvin's concept of predestination and election.

In 2 Peter 3:8, 9 Peter adds clarification to his earlier comments: "But do not forget this one thing, dear friends: With the Lord a day is like a thousand years, and a thousand years are like a day. The Lord is not slow in keeping his promise, as some understand slowness. He is patient with you, not wanting anyone to perish, but everyone to come to repentance." First, if God wants everyone to be saved, He could simply have predetermined it, since salvation is totally at His disposal. Second, if God has predetermined who is going to be saved and who is going to be lost, there is no need for Him to be patient, waiting to make sure that everybody has a chance to *decide* if they want to be saved.

God made His choice "before the creation of the world" (Ephesians 1:4). Choosing was part of His eternal plan. God's decision to redeem mankind and the methodology for doing so were set in place before the foundations of the world. God did not predetermine the individuals who would be redeemed. He predetermined the terms of redemption, which are "in Christ."

Notice that every one of the things from Ephesians 1 listed below are destined in Christ.

1. We should be "holy and blameless in his sight" (v. 4).
2. We should be "adopted" as children through Christ (v. 5).
3. Our "redemption . . . the forgiveness of sins" is in Him (v. 7).
4. God made known "the mystery of [H]is will" in Christ (v. 9).
5. We have been chosen in Christ (v. 11).
6. We are to live "for the praise of his glory" in Christ (v. 12).
7. We will be "marked" with the seal of the promised Holy Spirit in Him (v.13).

What is the significance of "in Christ"? How do we get "in Christ"? Are we in Christ by the predestined, arbitrary, and personal selection of God, or do we have to choose to do something to be in Christ? Look closely at the following passages. In Romans 6:3-5 Paul writes: "Or don't you know that all of us who were baptized into Christ Jesus were baptized into his death? We were therefore buried with him through baptism into death in order that, just as Christ was raised from the dead through the glory of the Father, we too may live a new life. If we have been united with him like this in his death, we will certainly also be united with him in his resurrection."

Again in Colossians 2:8-12 he writes

See to it that no one takes you captive through hollow and deceptive philosophy, which depends on human tradition and the basic principles of this world rather than on Christ. For in Christ all the fullness of the Deity lives in bodily form, and you have been given fullness in Christ, who is the head over every power and authority. In him you were also circumcised, in the putting off of the sinful nature, not with a circumcision done by the hands of men but with the circumcision done by Christ, having been buried with him in baptism and raised with him through your faith in the power of God, who raised him from the dead.

When Paul instructs the Christians in Colossae to "[s]ee to it" (Colossians 2:8), he means that they have something to do with the results. The words, "through your faith" (v. 12), place the responsibility on the saints in Colossae for all of God's work. Being "in Christ" is the result of a decision to be born again in baptism. The new birth is God's predestined condition, to being in Christ, but deciding to be obedient to that condition is a choice.

Now I want us to consider what Paul says in 2 Corinthians 5:20: "We are therefore Christ's ambassadors, as though God were making his appeal through us. We implore you on Christ's behalf: Be reconciled to God."

The idea of God "appealing" to us is a critical concept, because when you appeal to someone it necessarily implies that the person you are appealing to has the right to accept or reject the appeal. If God had predetermined specifically who the saved are, why would He "appeal" to them? Paul urges the Corinthians to "[b]e reconciled to God" (2 Corinthians 5:20). Being reconciled is something they must choose, and choosing is an act of the will.

A few other passages that add weight to this argument are

1. In 1 Peter 1:2, Peter says that we were "chosen ... for obedience." But obedience is a choice. If it is not voluntary, it is not obedience; it is servitude.

2. James mentions one in James 4:4 who "chooses to be a friend of the world."

3. In a familiar passage, Joshua tells the Israelites, "choose for yourselves this day whom you will serve" (Joshua 24:15).

In 2 Thessalonians 2:13, 14, Paul gives further evidence of what God's predestination means: "But we ought always to thank God for you, brothers loved by the Lord, because from the beginning God chose you to be saved through the sanctifying work of the Spirit and through belief in the truth. He called you to this through our gospel, that you might share in the glory of our Lord Jesus Christ."

Although Paul says in Ephesians 1:4 that God's choosing was "before the creation of the world"—which demonstrates the foreknowledge of God, as I have pointed out previously—His choosing was not the individuals that He was going to save, but the methodology by which they would be saved. There are two parts to that methodology.

The first part involves the sanctifying work of the Holy Spirit. But notice that the sanctifying work of the Holy Spirit is only effective with those who choose to accept that work. If the sanctifying work of the Holy Spirit was "irresistible," all people would be saved. In Stephen's sermon he says to those unbelieving Jews in Acts 7:51: "You stiff-necked people, with uncircumcised heart and ears! You are just like your fathers: You always resist the Holy Spirit!" That means that people have the power to choose to reject the sanctifying work of the Holy Spirit.

The second part of the methodology is through belief in the truth. But notice that belief is a choice. The choosing and the destining are generic. What God has chosen is a group of people. He has chosen them not based on His arbitrary whim but on their decision to choose Him.

Free will and predestination are not mutually exclusive. It is entirely probable that God has and continues to predestine certain events and people for His glory. Scripture cannot be correctly understood otherwise. See Joshua 11:20; Romans 11:7, 8; Romans 9:16-18.

The Holy Spirit says that God's choosing was "before the creation of the world" (Ephesians 1:4). God knew man was going to sin before He created him. It also means that God predetermined that He was going to redeem from sin every human being who wanted to be redeemed.

If God was going to redeem people, whether or not they wanted to be redeemed, then mankind would have had no choice in the matter; and there would have been no such thing as free will.

God's redemption is also based on our belief in the truth. Here is the part that people must play in their own redemption. They must choose to believe. God will not make that choice for us—indeed He cannot without defeating His own purposes.

God cannot be boxed in by arbitrary parameters of our choosing. He cannot be confined by our sense of justice, fair play, consistency, or logic. That is one of the main lessons from the book of Job. We must remember that God is absolutely sovereign. That means that He cannot be questioned. In Romans 9:19-21 Paul says that the clay does not say to the potter, "Why did you make me like this?" This illustration of God's absolute sovereignty might make us very uncomfortable if it were not for what we know about God's nature. God's nature is loving, kind, gracious, just, and merciful. We also know that He cannot act contrary to His nature. That means that He cannot act contrary to love, grace, mercy, and justice; which also means that everything He has done and continues to do must be placed in that light.

This discussion necessarily leads to the field of what we call "natural law." Isn't it true that God has set in place certain immutable "natural laws" by which He controls all the outcomes and circumstances of the universe? Are not those the laws that predetermine all of the events and circumstances of our lives? Does the concept of natural law not remove God from specific, personal responsibility for the circumstances of our lives?

One of the reasons for accepting the theory of natural law is the mental difficulty of conceiving a God who can continually juggle all the balls of the universe without getting tired, confused, or dropping one now and then. We commonly define a miracle as God's "supernatural intervention." Supernatural means above or beyond natural law. A miracle is defined as God either preventing something from happening or causing something to happen that changes what would have happened if His "natural laws" had been allowed to take their course. Under this view a prayer for safety in travel is a prayer for a miracle—asking God to prevent what would have happened if we had not prayed.

I would submit to you that God can operate the universe on a decision-by-decision basis, and it may be that what we call "natural law" is simply the result of infinite power and the actions of an infinitely ordered mind. But does He? Perhaps the question of *how* God runs the universe is moot. Perhaps it is simply beyond our ability to understand. But to believe that He *does* run the universe is critical to our faith. It is also critical that we not fall into the common unbelief that the universe is operated by some independent, unilateral system which functions outside of God's specific will and intent.

Natural law may simply be the terminology we have chosen which allows us to be more comfortable with the events of our lives. A hurricane or an earthquake that destroys towns and lives is somehow more tolerable if it results from natural law than if it is the result of the specific action and purpose of God.

Personally, I am more comfortable with the latter. I do not wish for any of the circumstances of my life to be the result of natural law, luck, or chance—the whim or caprice of a "lesser god" that is totally amoral, unfeeling, uncaring, and has no plan whatsoever.

Paul writes in 1 Corinthians 8:4-6: "So then, about eating food sacrificed to idols: We know that an idol is nothing at all in the world and that there is no God but one. For even if there are so-called gods, whether in heaven or on earth (as indeed there are many 'gods' and many 'lords'), yet for us there is but one God, the Father, from whom all things came and for whom we live; and there is but one Lord, Jesus Christ, through whom all things came and through whom we live."

Paul talks about the difference between what we know as Christians and what those who are not Christians know. One of the things we know is that God created and sustains the universe. Job says of God: "In his hand is the life of every creature and the breath of all mankind" (Job 12:10). "To God belong wisdom and power; counsel and understanding are his. What he tears down cannot be rebuilt; the man he imprisons cannot be released. If he holds back the waters, there is drought; if he lets them loose, they devastate the land. To him belong strength and victory; both deceived and deceiver are his" (vv.13-16). "He takes off the shackles put on by kings and ties a loincloth around their waist. He leads priests away stripped and overthrows men long established. He silences the lips of trusted advisers and takes away the discernment of elders" (vv.18-20). "He reveals the deep things of darkness and brings deep shadows into the light. He makes nations great, and destroys them; he enlarges nations, and disperses them. He deprives the leaders of the earth of their reason; he sends them wandering through a trackless waste" (vv. 22-24).

Was the book of Job written by inspiration? We must be careful how we answer. If it was not, the authenticity of the Bible is at stake.

If it was, then we must find a way to fit what it says about the personal involvement of God in virtually everything that happens into our ideas about providence.

Questions for 1 Peter 1:1, 2

1. Why does Peter refer to his audience as strangers scattered in the world?
2. What three foundational, but difficult, doctrines does Peter introduce to us in 1 Peter 1:1, 2?
3. Paul says that God "chose us [Christians]" (Ephesians 1:4). What does that mean?
4. Give three reasons why God "chose" us.
5. What does it mean to be "in Christ"?
6. What does predestine mean?
7. What exactly did God predestine before the foundations of the world?
8. Does the doctrine of predestination conflict with free will? Explain.
9. Look at and discuss the list in this chapter of things that are destined "in Christ."
10. Are we in Christ by the predestined selection of God, or do we have to *choose* to do something to be in Christ? If so, what do we have to choose?
11. God did not choose the *individuals* that He was going to save, but what did He choose?
12. What are the two parts to God's methodology for saving people?
13. Discuss some of the pros and cons of natural law.

Praise be to the God and Father of our Lord Jesus Christ! In his great mercy he has given us new birth into a living hope through the resurrection of Jesus Christ from the dead, and into an inheritance that can never perish, spoil or fade—kept in heaven for you, who through faith are shielded by God's power until the coming of the salvation that is ready to be revealed in the last time. In this you greatly rejoice, though now for a little while you may have had to suffer grief in all

kinds of trials. These have come so that your faith—of greater worth than gold, which perishes even though refined by fire—may be proved genuine and may result in praise, glory and honor when Jesus Christ is revealed. Though you have not seen him, you love him; and even though you do not see him now, you believe in him and are filled with an inexpressible and glorious joy, for you are receiving the goal of your faith, the salvation of your souls (1 Peter 1:3-9).

What is this "new birth"? (1 Peter 1:3). We learn from the conversation Jesus had with Nicodemus in John 3 that the new birth is what we receive when we are born again in baptism. In that new birth God grants us the gift of forgiveness of our sins and the reception of the indwelling Holy Spirit. They are both gifts because we receive them as an act of grace. We do not earn anything in baptism; we accept God's gifts.

In being born again, a "living hope" and a living Savior become ours because Jesus was raised from the dead (1 Peter 1:3). Salvation is ours because the new birth means that we are the children of God, and as a consequence of being His children we have an "inheritance" which is in the family mansion in heaven. Jesus promised His disciples that He would go and "prepare a place for you." He also promised: "In my Father's house are many rooms" (John 14:2). That place and those rooms are our inheritance.

First Peter 1:5 tells us that this new birth also means that we are shielded by faith. How are we shielded? Our shield of faith is not faith in ourselves; it is faith in God's power to deliver us from all harm and evil.

How does God's power impact our lives, and what is its source? Paul writes in Ephesians 3:14-21,

> For this reason I kneel before the Father, from whom his whole family in heaven and on earth derives its name. I pray that out of his glorious riches he may strengthen you with power through his Spirit in your inner being, so that Christ may dwell in your hearts through faith. And I pray that you, being rooted and established in love, may have power, together with all the saints, to grasp how wide and long and high and deep is the love of Christ, and to know this love that surpasses knowledge—that you may be filled to the measure of all the fullness of God. Now to him who is able to do immeasurably more than all we ask or imagine, according to his power that is at

work within us, to him be glory in the church and in Christ Jesus throughout all generations, for ever and ever! Amen.

God's power comes to us through the indwelling Holy Spirit. That power resides in our inner being. That inner being can be nothing but that spiritual nature which was created by the Holy Spirit in the new birth. (See John 3:1-8.) The role that our faith plays in being strengthened with power is fulfilled when we believe that God's Spirit indwells us.

What does the power given to us by the Holy Spirit do? It enlarges our heart, making it big enough to allow the Christ to dwell in it. The Holy Spirit also empowers us to "grasp" (Ephesians 3:18)—to get our hearts, minds, and souls around the entire circumference of the love of the indwelling Christ. The human heart simply isn't big enough to contain the risen Christ. ("Heart" here refers to the emotional capacity to understand and appreciate.) Without the Holy Spirit, Jesus may occasionally influence our lives, but the indwelling Holy Spirit enables Him to live there—to take up residence and become a permanent fixture. The Holy Spirit accomplishes this incredible feat by giving us the experience—the knowing of the love of the Christ. Without His indwelling, the human mind and emotions simply cannot come to grips with that love.

The Christ indwells us "through faith" (Ephesians 3:17). But that faith is in the power that the indwelling Holy Spirit brings. It is *only* because the risen Christ dwells in us by faith that we have the strength to overcome sin. The reason we are able to do that is because we are so full of Jesus that there is no room for our selfish nature or Satan to operate. Our duty as Christians is not to focus on ridding ourselves of the sinful things in our lives as much as it is to focus on so filling ourselves with the Christ that there is no room for Satan to get a foothold in us.

Think about Jesus' parable in Luke 11:24-26 about the evil spirit who came out of a man and wandered through waterless places. Finding no rest it returned to its original home and found it "swept clean and put in order" (v. 25). The evil spirit then went and found seven spirits worse than itself, and they went and lived there. This man emptied himself of bad habits, but he failed to fill himself with good ones and ended up worse than when he started.

What does our faith in the power of God "shield" us from? Paul says in Ephesians 6:16: "[T]ake up the shield of faith, with which you can extinguish all the flaming arrows of the evil one." The shield of faith will protect us from Satan's schemes until we no longer need it—when Jesus returns.

We rejoice in "the salvation that is ready to be revealed in the last time" (1 Peter 1:5). What is going to be revealed? The church triumphant is going to be revealed with God's justice and righteousness. Jesus will be proclaimed as King of kings and Lord of lords.

Peter says that trials come to us so that our faith may be "proved genuine" and so that God may be praised (1 Peter 1:7). There is no way for our faith to be tested except through trials. James writes, "Consider it pure joy, my brothers, whenever you face trials of many kinds, because you know that the testing of your faith develops perseverance. Perseverance must finish its work so that you may be mature and complete, not lacking anything" (James 1:2-4). God both causes and allows trials to come so that our faith can be "refined" and "proved genuine" (1 Peter 1:7).

God caused Joseph, Abraham, Moses, Esther, and Hannah to be tested and tried in order that their faith could be "proved genuine." I would urge you to think of those you know whose faith has proved genuine. It is a well-known fact of life that there is a direct relationship between the value that we placed on something and the price we had to pay for it. A great marriage is purchased at a great price. If something as wonderful as salvation, forgiveness, or righteousness came easily, we would not value it. An untested faith is a weak faith. In fact, we can never be certain that we have faith until it is tested.

Trials do not deprive us of "inexpressible" joy (1 Peter 1:8). How is it possible to be joyful in trial? Christians are not masochists who delight in pain. We delight in what the trial leads to. Peter says in 1 Peter 1:9: "[F]or you are receiving the goal of your faith." That goal is "the salvation of your souls." Hebrews 12:2 says that the Christ "who for the joy set before him endured the cross, scorning its shame." The joy was not in the cross but in the anticipation of accomplishing the will of God.

Questions for 1 Peter 1:3-9

1. What is this "new birth" that God has given us?

2. If it is a "gift," does that mean that we don't have to "do" anything?

3. How are we shielded by faith?

4. How does God's power impact our lives, and what is the source of that power?

5. What does the power do that is given to us by the Holy Spirit?

6. Give at least two reasons why trials come to us.

7. How is it possible to be joyful in trial?

Concerning this salvation, the prophets, who spoke of the grace that was to come to you, searched intently and with the greatest care, trying to find out the time and circumstances to which the Spirit of Christ in them was pointing when he predicted the sufferings of Christ and the glories that would follow. It was revealed to them that they were not serving themselves but you, when they spoke of the things that have now been told you by those who have preached the gospel to you by the Holy Spirit sent from heaven. Even angels long to look into these things (1 Peter 1:10-12).

What did the "Spirit of Christ" predict? He predicted the "sufferings" and the "glories" of the Christ (1 Peter 1:11). The sufferings are described by Isaiah in 53:1-6,

Who has believed our message and to whom has the arm of the LORD been revealed? He grew up before him like a tender shoot, and like a root out of dry ground. He had no beauty or majesty to attract us to him, nothing in his appearance that we should desire him. He was despised and rejected by men, a man of sorrows, and familiar with suffering. Like one from whom men hide their faces he was despised, and we esteemed him not. Surely he took up our infirmities and carried our sorrows, yet we considered him stricken by God, smitten by him, and afflicted. But he was pierced for our transgressions, he was crushed for our iniquities; the punishment that brought us peace was upon him, and by his wounds we are healed. We all, like sheep, have gone astray, each of us has turned to his own way; and the LORD has laid on him the iniquity of us all.

The "glories" of the Christ are described by Isaiah in 9:6, 7: "For to us a child is born, to us a son is given, and the government will be on his shoulders. And he will be called Wonderful Counselor, Mighty God,

Everlasting Father, Prince of Peace. Of the increase of his government and peace there will be no end. He will reign on David's throne and over his kingdom, establishing and upholding it with justice and righteousness from that time on and forever. The zeal of the LORD Almighty will accomplish this."

The prophets knew that they would never experience personally the things they were predicting and preaching about. All subsequent generations are the beneficiaries of the faith of those who have gone before us. Those great men of the Bible never saw what we see; they never experienced what we have the privilege of receiving. Can you imagine the curiosity they must have had about the things they were predicting and how they might have longed to see them firsthand?

First Peter 1:12 speaks of "things that have now been told you by those who have preached the gospel to you by the Holy Spirit sent from heaven." How was the gospel "preached ... by the Holy Spirit sent from heaven"? The apostles were inspired by the Holy Spirit to preach. They were told what to say and where to go; just how the Holy Spirit did that, we do not always know. We do know that sometimes it was done in visions, as with Peter and Paul. Perhaps sometimes it was done by guiding their thoughts as they spoke or wrote. In Luke 12:11, 12 Jesus says to His disciples: "When you are brought before synagogues, rulers and authorities, do not worry about how you will defend yourselves or what you will say, for the Holy Spirit will teach you at that time what you should say."

"Even angels long to look into these things" (1 Peter 1:12). It may come as a surprise to us to learn that the angels do not know all things. Verses like this one pique our curiosity, and we often wish that we knew more. Obviously, if we needed to know more, God would have told us.

Questions for 1 Peter 1:10-12

1. What did the "Spirit of Christ" predict?
2. Discuss this statement: "All subsequent generations are the beneficiaries of the faith of those who have gone before us."
3. How was the gospel "preached...by the Holy Spirit sent from heaven"?

Therefore, prepare [gird] your minds for action; be self-controlled; set your hope fully on the grace to be given you when Jesus Christ is revealed. As obedient children, do not conform to the evil desires you had when you lived in ignorance. But just as he who called you is holy, so be holy in all you do; for it is written: "Be holy, because I am holy" (1 Peter 1:13-16).

"Therefore" means that what the writer is about to say is based on what he has just said. "Therefore, prepare your minds for action." We must be prepared for the trials, temptations, and opportunities that are before us. We must not revert to the materialistic thinking and actions we had before we gave our lives to Christ.

"[P]repare" or "gird" (NKJV). The girdle was an essential article of dress in the East for both men and women. It served as a type of belt, but it had a multitude of other purposes. We are told in 2 Kings 1:8 that "[Elijah] was an hairy man, and *girt* with a girdle of leather" (KJV). These girdles were used to hold in the loose folds of cloth that characterized most of their garments and gave them shape. (More modern girdles were designed to hold in other things and give shape to people.) When a man or woman needed to move quickly, they tucked the lower portion of their robes into their girdle.

"Prepare your minds for action" is a statement of excitement (1 Peter 1:13). "Get ready to run," Peter says. Would you say that *you* were ready for action, or would you say that you were comfortable? Would you describe your spiritual state as excited or complacent? Of course, you know the right answer, but is there *evidence* in your life to bear witness to what you say?

"[B]e self-controlled; set your hope fully on the grace to be given you" (1 Peter 1:13). Our hope for redemption, peace, joy, courage, faithfulness, overcoming temptation, patience—for every Christian virtue—is based completely on the reconciliation extended to us through the cross.

Peter adds to the ancient grace-works tension by immediately adding, "As obedient children" (1 Peter 1:14). How do I set my hope fully on grace if I am to be judged by my obedience? The best resolution to that tension is to understand that the only appropriate response to a gift (and grace is a gift) is gratitude, and gratitude is best demonstrated by our actions—in this case obedience to the One who extends grace to us. Our obedience is not out of a sense of duty or obligation, but as a demonstration of gratitude.

We need also to remember that Jesus said if we, the branches, abide in Him, the vine, we cannot help but "bear fruit" (John 15:4, 5). That fruit is the good works that naturally result from remaining in the vine.

"But just as he who called you is holy, so be holy in all you do; for it is written: 'Be holy, because I am holy' " (1 Peter 1:15, 16). Peter tells us in 1 Peter 1:14, 15 that as God's children, we inherit the qualities of our Parent. God's nature is holy.

In baptism we were "born again" into the family of God. We became His children, and we are to conduct ourselves according to our new nature which is "holiness." In that new birth the "divine nature"—the divine attribute of holiness—was passed to us genetically. Paul tells us in Romans 6:2 that we also "died to sin" in the new birth. In Romans 8 we learn that God, through the indwelling Spirit, put to death the sinful nature and in the same process empowered us to put on holiness. Holy is what we are becoming, and good works are the outgrowth of holiness. As we take on the image of our Father we grow to be like Him. Being holy has to do with our search to know our Father. The more we know of Him the more like Him we become. As we learned in 1 Peter 1:2, holiness is the result of the Spirit's work in us.

Questions for 1 Peter 1:13-16

1. What does the word "therefore" usually mean when it appears in New Testament writings?
2. Why should we "[p]repare our minds for action"?
3. Would you say that you are ready for action or would you say that you are comfortable, excited, or complacent?
4. How can we set our hope *fully* on grace if we are to be judged by our obedience?
5. How do we obtain the divine attribute of holiness?

Since you call on a Father who judges each man's work impartially, live your lives as strangers here in reverent fear. For you know that it was not with perishable things such as silver or gold that you were redeemed from the empty way of life handed down to you from your forefathers, but with the precious blood of Christ, a lamb without blemish or defect. He was chosen before the creation of the world,

CHAPTER 1

but was revealed in these last times for your sake. Through him you believe in God, who raised him from the dead and glorified him, and so your faith and hope are in God. (1 Peter 1:17-21).

God "judges each man's work impartially." The fact that God is going to have an impartial judgment should provide the impetus for living "in reverent fear" (1 Peter 1:17). Reverent fear is not characterized by the abject, mortal terror one feels when confronted by an amoral, unfeeling, tyrannical ruling despot. Reverent fear is the attitude of awe, reverence, and deep respect inspired by an all-powerful, all-knowing, loving, patient, forgiving, gracious, merciful but wrathful, just, and jealous God.

He will judge our work "impartially" (1 Peter 1:17). What does that mean? If we are saved by grace, why are our works going to be judged? And not only "judged," but judged impartially? We read in Revelation 20:12: "And I saw the dead, great and small, standing before the throne, and books were opened. Another book was opened, which is the book of life. The dead were judged according to what they had done as recorded in the books." Make no mistake; the deeds we have done on this earth play a critical role in how God judges us.

Paul writes in 1 Corinthians 3:10-15,

> By the grace God has given me, I laid a foundation as an expert builder, and someone else is building on it. But each one should be careful how he builds. For no one can lay any foundation other than the one already laid, which is Jesus Christ. If any man builds on this foundation using gold, silver, costly stones, wood, hay or straw, his work will be shown for what it is, because the Day will bring it to light. It will be revealed with fire, and the fire will test the quality of each man's work. If what he has built survives, he will receive his reward. If it is burned up, he will suffer loss; he himself will be saved, but only as one escaping through the flames.

Our works are the measure of our faith. They measure the degree to which we have accepted the grace of God and the gift of salvation, and have taken advantage of the power resident in us through the indwelling Holy Spirit. If the grace of God, the gift of salvation, and the reception of the Holy Spirit have made no measurable impact on the way we live, think, and act, that is evidence that they have not had the impact on our lives that God intended; and He will judge us "impartially" (1 Peter 1:17).

Our works are the evidence of our degree of sanctification and holiness. In Galatians 5:16-26 Paul contrasts what the Spirit produces when we live according to His leading with what the flesh produces when we live according to its leading.

So I say, live by the Spirit, and you will not gratify the desires of the sinful nature. For the sinful nature desires what is contrary to the Spirit, and the Spirit what is contrary to the sinful nature. They are in conflict with each other, so that you do not do what you want. But if you are led by the Spirit, you are not under law. The acts of the sinful nature are obvious: sexual immorality, impurity and debauchery; idolatry and witchcraft; hatred, discord, jealousy, fits of rage, selfish ambition, dissentions, factions and envy; drunkenness, orgies, and the like. I warn you, as I did before, that those who live like this will not inherit the kingdom of God. But the fruit of the Spirit is love, joy, peace, patience, kindness, goodness, faithfulness, gentleness and self-control. Against such things there is no law. Those who belong to Christ Jesus have crucified the sinful nature with its passions and desires. Since we live by the Spirit, let us keep in step with the Spirit. Let us not become conceited, provoking and envying each other.

What does it mean to "live by the Spirit" (Galatians 5:16)? It means to acknowledge His indwelling. It means to listen to His leading and obey His convicting work. The fruit of the Spirit measures the extent to which we have allowed Him to influence our lives. If we are living by the Spirit, then the fruit of the Spirit (v. 22, 23) will be evidenced in our lives. If that fruit is missing, it means that we have quenched the Spirit of God and therefore have placed ourselves in danger of being lost.

Questions for 1 Peter 1:17-21

1. What is "reverent fear" (1 Peter 1:17)?
2. Would you say that you have reverent fear?
3. What does it mean that God will judge our works "impartially"?
4. If we are saved by grace, why are our works going to be judged? And not only judged but judged "impartially"?
5. What do our works measure?
6. What does it mean to "live by the Spirit"? Would you say that you are living that way? How? Why?

Now that you have purified yourselves by obeying the truth so that you have sincere love for your brothers, love one another deeply, from the heart. For you have been born again, not of perishable seed, but of imperishable, through the living and enduring word of God. For, "All men are like grass, and all their glory is like the flowers of the field; the grass withers and the flowers fall, but the word of the Lord stands forever." And this is the word that was preached to you (1 Peter 1:22-25)

Obedience to the truth leads to the purification of our souls. The key words here are obedience, truth, purification, and soul. The importance of obedience is stressed by Paul in Romans 6:16-18: "Don't you know that when you offer yourselves to someone to obey him as slaves, you are slaves to the one whom you obey—whether you are slaves to sin, which leads to death, or to obedience, which leads to righteousness? But thanks be to God that, though you used to be slaves to sin, you wholeheartedly obeyed the form of teaching to which you were entrusted. You have been set free from sin and have become slaves to righteousness."

Obedience is essential to having a relationship with God. It indicates submission, the recognition of authority, and the conquering of our pride. Philippians 2:8 says that the Christ "became obedient" to death. The Christ "learned obedience" through suffering (Hebrews 5:8). The truth must be *obeyed* in order for it to have any meaning in our lives. Truth is useless to us unless it leads to obedience.

Obedience is more than acceptance. Obedience is acquiescence and action. By obedience we place ourselves in subjection to the one we obey. The irony is that submissive obedience to God's truth leads to personal freedom. But we do not free ourselves by obedience; we are freed by the risen Christ.

In Christianity there is one great, all-consuming truth. That truth is not *about* Jesus; it *is* Jesus. The answer to Pilate's question "What is truth?" (John 18:38) is that Jesus *is* the truth. There are no truths in this universe that are not found in the resurrected Christ. When we obey the truth, we obey Jesus. We sing the words, "Where He leads me I will follow." We sing, "Trust and obey, for there's no other way." Yes, it is easy to sing those words. The real challenge is, are we ready to do it?

Purified. There are two basic understandings of purity. The first is the absence of foreign material, as in pure gold, pure luck, and pure skill. The second is singleness of purpose, as in "seek first [the] kingdom"

(Matthew 6:33). In this passage the second of these is most appropriate. Our sincere love for each other is not divided by other loyalties or obligations. This love is internally motivated by the most basic part of our being, our souls. The soul is responsible for our higher longings. When the soul is devoted to the right qualities it is a powerful force in the decision making process.

Our dedication to each other is tied directly to our obedience to the truth (1 Peter 1:22). John says that "We love because he first loved us" (1 John 4:19). The care, concern, patience, and kindness that Christians extend to each other is the result of their obedience to the truth. We are to love one another fervently, not from selfish motivations, but from the heart. We love in this way because we have been "born again" into the family of God. The results of our new birth create family feelings that overpower selfishness and pride.

In 1 Peter 1:23 Peter tells us that our new birth is "not of perishable seed," but imperishable seed. That means that unlike our natural birth, our new birth does not lead inevitably to death, but to life. Paul gives us great insight into what this new birth leads to when he writes in 1 Corinthians 15:35, 36, 42-44: "But someone may ask, 'How are the dead raised? With what kind of body will they come?' How foolish! What you sow does not come to life unless it dies...The body that is sown is perishable, it is raised imperishable; it is sown in dishonor, it is raised in glory; it is sown in weakness, it is raised in power; it is sown a natural body, it is raised a spiritual body."

"[T]he word of the Lord stands forever" (1 Peter 1:25). We have been born again through the living and abiding Word of God. This is the Word which we preach. Obey the Word, purify your soul, take your place in the family of God, and lay hold on eternal life.

Questions for 1 Peter 1:22-25

1. What is the relationship between obedience and purification?
2. What is the irony in submissive obedience to God's truth?
3. In Christianity there is one great, all-consuming truth. What is that truth?
4. What are the two basic understandings of purity?
5. What does it mean to be born of imperishable seed?

FIRST PETER
CHAPTER 2

Therefore, rid yourselves of all malice and all deceit, hypocrisy, envy, and slander of every kind. Like newborn babies, crave pure spiritual milk, so that by it you may grow up in your salvation, now that you have tasted that the Lord is good (1 Peter 2:1-3).

"Therefore" always refers to what has just been said. It is the same as "because." In this case it is: Because you have been "born again" of imperishable seed. Because you have taken on the "divine nature." Because you are a "new creation." Because of these things—"Therefore" you must stop acting like your old man of sin was in control. You must stop loving the world and living according to its standards of success, meaning, and value.

The command to "rid yourselves" means to make a conscious decision and take action. Have you made that decision? Can you point to specific things in your life that would demonstrate your decision?

What sins are we to rid ourselves of? The sins enumerated here are what I would refer to as "sins of the disposition." Although there may be external actions associated with these sins, it is not those actions that constitute the problem—it is the internal condition that *caused* the action that is the problem. Human initiative may be sufficient to keep us from committing the external actions, but only the indwelling Holy Spirit can empower us to put to death the internal disposition that motivates them. Notice also that everything we are to rid ourselves of has it roots in pride.

The human tendency is to focus on the external manifestation of sin. Jesus focused on the internal condition that led to the sin. In the Sermon on the Mount, Jesus says that anger (the internal condition) is the cause of murder (the external action), and lust (the internal condition) is the cause of adultery (the external action) (Matthew 5:21, 22, 27-30). God is more concerned with the heart than with the hands because the hands only perform the intentions of the heart. We will never stop sinning until we stop *wanting* to sin.

In Matthew 15:10-20 Matthew records

> Jesus called the crowd to him and said, "Listen and understand. What goes into a man's mouth does not make him 'unclean,' but what comes out of his mouth, that is what makes him 'unclean.'" Then the disciples came to him and asked, "Do you know that the Pharisees were offended when they heard this?" He replied, "Every plant that my heavenly Father has not planted will be pulled up by the roots. Leave them; they are blind guides. If a blind man leads a blind man, both will fall into a pit." Peter said, "Explain the parable to us." "Are you still so dull?" Jesus asked them. "Don't you see that whatever enters the mouth goes into the stomach and then out of the body? But the things that come out of the mouth come from the heart, and these make a man 'unclean.' For out of the heart come evil thoughts, murder, adultery, sexual immorality, theft, false testimony, slander. These are what make a man 'unclean'; but eating with unwashed hands does not make him 'unclean.'

Why were the Pharisees offended? Because their whole emphasis was on fulfilling the external, legal requirements of the law.

Sins of the disposition are not only much harder to deal with than sins of the flesh; they are much harder to admit. This can be illustrated with the story of the prodigal son and his older brother in Luke 15. Consider carefully the following points:

1. The prodigal son's first sin was one of the disposition; he rebelled against his father. All of the other sins he committed were sins of the flesh.
2. The older brother commited no sins of the flesh that we are aware of. All of his sins were sins of the disposition, and virtually every one of them was rooted in pride. There are a few things in the narrative that might lead us to believe that the reason he was so angry with his brother was that his brother actually did what he had always wanted to do, but lacked the courage to do.
3. In the "distant country" the prodigal son "came to his senses." He saw himself for exactly what he was. Please notice that the only reason he came to himself was because of his suffering.

4. Why do you suppose that the elder brother never "came to his senses"? Consider the possibility that it was because he stayed where it was safe; therefore he never suffered. Consider also that it was because his sins were sins of the disposition rather than of the flesh. He was jealous, prideful, angry, and spiteful.

5. The story ends with the prodigal welcomed back home, understanding grace, and being at peace with his father. He was penitent, humble, forgiven, and joyful because he *knew* that he was unworthy.

6. The story ends with his older brother outside, steeped in his pride, angry, unhappy, frustrated, alienated from his father, and believing that he had been treated unfairly. He had no joy. He experienced no forgiveness because he lacked the humility that would have made him aware that he needed it. He had no understanding of grace because he wanted only what he thought he deserved.

We can safely conclude that sins of the disposition are much easier to detect in others than in ourselves. Consider the following questions:

1. Do you think you are most guilty of sins of the flesh or sins of disposition?

2. Which son do you think ends up better off?

3. Which son would you rather be?

4. The answers to the first three questions are pretty easy. The next question is more difficult. Would you be willing to pay the price the prodigal son paid to be where he ended up?

We all want to rid ourselves of the sins that Peter mentions, but we cannot rid ourselves of sins that we refuse to confess. Christianity is not a religion that focuses on what we are not. If the focus of our preaching and teaching is on getting rid of bad habits, we will never succeed. Christianity focuses on the positive aspects of filling ourselves. We have to be focused on being so full of the Holy Spirit and the risen Christ that there is no room left for sin to get a foothold.

In order to rid ourselves of what is undesirable, we have to start craving what is desirable. In Peter's words, "pure spiritual milk" leads to sanctification, a deeper and more personal relationship with God, deeper spiritual goals, and a deeper knowledge of the Word (1 Peter 2:2).

What is "pure spiritual milk"? The "milk" is the Word of God. It seems to me that one of the appropriate applications of this passage for us today is that we should spend more time with the Bible and less time with books about the Bible. People are always asking me if I have read certain books. They say, "You just have to read this book; it changed my life!" I can't remember anyone ever coming up to me and with great excitement saying, "Have you read the second chapter of Romans recently? It changed my life!"

Would you say that you enjoy Bible study? Do you find yourself anticipating discussion of the Word? I don't mean talking about the Word but getting into the Word. I realize that a person can know much about the Bible and not know God, but we must also realize that we will never come to know God without diligently studying His Word.

Are you intrigued by trite, superficial, and self-serving books like *The Prayer of Jabez* and *Left Behind*? Peter says that the Word helps us "grow up in [our] salvation" (1 Peter 2:2). The purpose of study, spiritual discussion, and introspection is not to gain religious information, but spiritual growth.

How can we grow in respect to salvation? It's a fascinating concept. We are prone to think of salvation as something static—either you are or you aren't. And although there is truth in that, there has to be an aspect of salvation that is progressive or we could not "grow" in respect to it.

Jesus presents an expanded concept of eternal life, heaven, and salvation in John 17:3 when He says, "Now this is eternal life: that they may know you, the only true God, and Jesus Christ, whom you have sent."

Let me challenge your thinking with this brief illustration. If a couple has a baby and it dies at the age of six months, we understand that they could not possibly have the depth of love for it that they would have had if the baby had lived long enough for them to *know* it better.

If eternal life is equated with knowing God—and Jesus says that it is—there has to be a spiritual sense in which we can become more "saved" as we come to know God more perfectly. I would like to challenge you with this possibility. Does that mean that some people are more saved than others, and some are more lost than others?

These two passages indicate very strongly that this is the case. Jesus says in Luke 12:47, 48: "That servant who knows his master's will and does not get ready or does not do what his master wants will be beaten with many blows. But the one who does not know and does things deserving punishment will be beaten with few blows." However we translate "blows," it certainly means that some people are going to suffer more than others.

Paul tells us in 1 Corinthians 3:13-15 that "the fire will test the quality of each man's work. If what he has built survives, he will receive his reward. If it is burned up, he will suffer loss; he himself will be saved, but only as one escaping through the flames." I can see no way to avoid, and I don't know why we would want to avoid the conclusion from these words, that some people are "more saved" than others. We may say that we would be happy to be saved at the lowest level possible; but we know that is not God's purpose, and it should not be ours.

The parable that Jesus teaches in Matthew 20:1-16 about the laborers who are hired at different times receiving the same reward certainly indicates that the reward we receive will not be based on how *long* we work in His kingdom, but on God's determination of the *value* of our service.

> So when those came who were hired first, they expected to receive more. But each one of them also received a denarius. When they received it, they began to grumble against the landowner. 'These men who were hired last worked only one hour,' they said, 'and you have made them equal to us who have borne the burden of the work and the heat of the day.' But he answered one of them, 'Friend, I am not being unfair to you. Didn't you agree to work for a denarius? Take your pay and go. I want to give the man who was hired last the same as I gave you. Don't I have the right to do what I want with my own money? Or are you envious because I am generous?' So the last will be first, and the first will be last (vs. 10-16).

Although there are several lessons in this parable, we must always be looking for the intent for which Jesus told it rather than incidental aspects of the story. Here's a synopsis: Jesus deliberately sets up the story so that those hired first were paid last. Normally it would be the opposite. That tells us something about the purpose of the parable. The first laborers agreed to work for a specific amount, a denarius. The other workers agreed to work for "whatever is right." When those hired first saw that those hired last received what they had agreed to work for, they supposed they would receive more. Their "grumbling" indicates that they thought they deserved more.

The intent of the parable is revealed in the master's statement in Matthew 20:15: "Don't I have the right to do what I want with my own money? Or are you envious because I am generous?" The point of the parable is that it is God's salvation, and He has the right to give it to whomever He pleases on whatever basis pleases Him.

I suspect that the main reason Jesus told the parable had to do with making a point about the Jew-Gentile aspect of salvation. The Jews thought of themselves as the chosen ones and all others as second class. They supposed that God would be more favorably disposed toward them and reward them more richly because they had been His people for a much longer time and had suffered more—four hundred years of bondage in Egypt, forty years wandering in the wilderness, fighting to win the Promised Land, and much, much more.

When Peter urges Christians in 1 Peter 2:2 to "crave pure spiritual milk, so that *by it* you may grow up in your salvation," he may have in mind growing up in our understanding of salvation, as well as growing up in the Christian graces, in the fruit of the Spirit, and in our knowledge of and appreciation for God.

What is "pure spiritual milk"? As mentioned above, the "milk" is the Bible—the Word of God. "Pure milk" is the Word of God that is not contaminated or watered down by human interpretation, thought, or prejudice. Peter says that if we *crave* this milk, we will grow. All growth is painful because it means *change*. Physical growth takes place naturally because God created us with the physical capacity for growth. If we eat, sleep, and exercise, we will grow. The same is true spiritually. God meant for us to grow spiritually, and He created us with the capacity for it. But we must eat, sleep, and exercise spiritually in order for it to happen.

Spiritual growth is measured by our knowledge of God. Paul says, "I want to know Christ" (Philippians 3:10). He doesn't mean know about Christ; he means that he wants to experience Christ, to see what He saw and to feel what He felt and to love God the way He loved God. We get married because we want to know someone better. We may not always like what we find out, but that too is part of the learning experience.

We will grow if we eat the right things. Remember Jesus told the disciples in John 4:32: "I have food to eat that you know nothing about." What food was He talking about? His food was to do the will of God. Our food is to eat His flesh and drink His blood (6:53-56).

Questions for 1 Peter 2:1-3

1. Peter tells his audience to rid themselves of some sinful practices. That means that they had to make a conscious decision and take action.

Have you made that decision? Can you point to specific things in your life that would demonstrate it?

2. What is the difference between sins of the flesh and sins of the disposition?

3. Discuss this statement: We will never stop sinning until we stop *wanting* to sin.

4. In the story of the prodigal son, why do you suppose that the elder brother never comes to his senses?

5. What is the intent of the parable of the laborers?

6. What is "pure spiritual milk"?

7. Peter says that we must "grow up in [our] salvation." If salvation is only something static—either you are or you are not—how is it possible to "grow" in it?

8. How is spiritual growth measured?

As you come to him, the living Stone—rejected by men but chosen by God and precious to him—you also, like living stones, are being built into a spiritual house to be a holy priesthood, offering spiritual sacrifices acceptable to God through Jesus Christ. For in Scripture it says: "See, I lay a stone in Zion, a chosen and precious cornerstone, and the one who trusts in him will never be put to shame." Now to you who believe, this stone is precious. But to those who do not believe, "The stone the builders rejected has become the capstone," and, "A stone that causes men to stumble and a rock that makes them fall." They stumble because they disobey the message—which is also what they were destined for (1 Peter 2:4-8).

Notice the words "are being built" (1 Peter 2:5). That present tense indicates an ongoing process. The "spiritual house" is the kingdom of God, the church. There are two groups mentioned: builders and believers. The "builders" undoubtedly refer to the Jews who rejected Jesus as the Messiah because they were totally focused on having a material kingdom.

The Jews rejected the foundation—cornerstone—that God intended to use for what He was building which was the Christ and His gospel. The "believers" are those who are building on the "rock," the Christ

Himself who is the cornerstone, the foundation of their building; and that building is the church.

The children of God are the stones, not the builders. They do not build the kingdom; God does that. That has far-reaching implications for the attitude we manifest when we proclaim the gospel.

In the process of coming to Him, which has to do with accepting Jesus as the Christ and the Lord of our lives, God begins to use His children as "building blocks" in His house, which is the church. His children serve as "holy priests" who offer "spiritual sacrifices." The spiritual sacrifices are the "presentation of their bodies" on a daily basis.

Internally, that presentation consists of the "fruit of the Spirit" that are listed in Galatians 5. Externally, that presentation consists of the sanctified lives that proclaim our faith and result in the proclamation of the gospel. Christians, as a "holy priesthood"—a people "sanctified to God" and to His purposes—emanate His presence from within—in the form of "rivers of living water" because of the indwelling Holy Spirit. The result is that we are never "ashamed" of our faith, our morality, or our values.

The Christ is the resurrected, living cornerstone and the foundation upon which the entire "spiritual house," the kingdom of God, rests. "To [those] who believe" Christ is precious because He is the source of comfort, forgiveness, peace, hope, and salvation. To those "who do not believe," Christ is the enemy. What was intended by God to be a blessing—to extend hope of everlasting life—has become a message of despair and condemnation.

Paul writes in 2 Corinthians 2:14-16: "But thanks be to God, who always leads us in triumphal procession in Christ and through us spreads everywhere the fragrance of the knowledge of him. For we are to God the aroma of Christ among those who are being saved and those who are perishing. To the one we are the smell of death; to the other, the fragrance of life. And who is equal to such a task?" Unbelievers stumble because of the message (1 Peter 2:8). What is that message?

1. "[I]f you do not believe that I am the one I claim to be, you will indeed die in your sins" (John 8:24).

2. "But small is the gate and narrow the road that leads to life, and only a few find it" (Matthew 7:14).

3. "No one comes to the Father except through me" (John 14:6).

We need to remember how clearly defined the line is between believers and unbelievers as far as God is concerned. We want so badly to believe that there is some "middle ground" for those who are "good people." It is an illusion! It is one of Satan's favorite tools to deceive those who are not schooled in the Scriptures.

It needs to be noted, in view of our study of predestination in chapter 1, that just as the believers are predestined to everlasting life, unbelievers are predestined to everlasting condemnation in hell. "They stumble because they disobey the message" (1 Peter 2:8). But remember that disobedience is a choice. And what is the message? Essentially it is "unless you repent, you too will all perish" (Luke 13:3).

Questions for 1 Peter 2:4-8

1. What is the spiritual house that God is building?

2. What role do Christians play in that house?

3. What are the "spiritual sacrifices" that Christians contribute to that house?

4. What is there about the message of the cross that causes people to stumble?

5. Why is it important to us that there be an acceptable "middle ground" between believers and non-believers?

But you are a chosen people, a royal priesthood, a holy nation, a people belonging to God, that you may declare the praises of him who called you out of darkness into his wonderful light. Once you were not a people, but now you are the people of God; once you had not received mercy, but now you have received mercy (1 Peter 2:9, 10).

Each of the descriptive terms that Peter uses for Christians has a significance of its own. Peter intendes these adjectives to be an encouragement to the persecuted Christians to whom he writes. He reminds them that being under covenant with God has privileges and blessings as well as hardships.

The term "chosen people" is especially encouraging because it is personal. God has not chosen us at random or even collectively. He has chosen us specifically and personally. Christians are "a royal priesthood." As God's priests we have special intercessory opportunities because God is especially interested in the requests of His children. We are to offer up thanksgiving and praise to our Father as well as petitions for the physical and spiritual needs and sins of others.

James 5:13-16: "Is any one of you in trouble? He should pray. Is anyone happy? Let him sing songs of praise. Is any one of you sick? He should call the elders of the church to *pray over him* and anoint him with oil in the name of the Lord. And the prayer offered in faith will make the sick person well; the Lord will raise him up. If he has sinned, he will be forgiven. Therefore confess your sins to each other and pray for each other so that you may be healed."

"[A] holy nation" (1 Peter 2:9). Christians are a people who are sanctified to God and focused on one thing: knowing Him and seeking first His kingdom. Christians belong to God. We are owned by God because He has purchased us by paying the price of our redemption—the blood of His Son Jesus. What an exalted privilege and honor and what consolation and encouragement it brings to know that because God cannot be defeated, we cannot be defeated.

But we were not simply chosen; we were chosen *to be* something. We were chosen that we might "declare." It's like being chosen to play on an athletic team. We are not chosen to be a "bench warmer." We are chosen to play, and not only to play, but to play a certain position - the position for which we are gifted - so that we can contribute to the team's success. It is good also to remember that we are not chosen because we are great, or because of any talent or merit we possess. We were chosen by grace and because of what God can make out of us.

Questions for 1 Peter 2:9, 10

1. What does the term "chosen people" mean to Christians?
2. How does God choose us?
3. What does the term "holy nation" mean to Christians?
4. What were we chosen to be?

Dear friends, I urge you, as aliens and strangers in the world, to abstain from sinful desires, which war against your soul. Live such good lives among the pagans that, though they accuse you of doing wrong, they may see your good deeds and glorify God on the day he visits us (1 Peter 2:11, 12).

Because we are a holy nation and a royal priesthood we are also "aliens and strangers." Our hope is not in this life. Paul reminds the Corinthian congregation in 1 Corinthians 15:19, "If only for this life we have hope in Christ, we are to be pitied more than all men."

Because we do not see ourselves as only going around once, we need to regard this life through eyes that see this world not as an *end*, but as the *means* to the end, which is everlasting life with God. As Christians we must understand that what we see with our human eyes is a very small part of reality.

Our view of the world is similar to an iceberg. Only ten percent of an iceberg is above the surface and seen. The ninety percent that is below the surface is just as real as the ten percent above the surface. It takes a special pair of eyes to see what is beneath the surface, and you have to be looking for it.

This material world is only ten percent of reality. The ninety percent world of spiritual reality is just as real, but it is only seen through spiritual eyes that are powered by faith. The human tendency is to focus our efforts on the ten percent reality that our physical eyes perceive as *reality*, because we think we can impact that.

In 1 Peter 2:11 Peter encourages Christians to "abstain from sinful desires, which war against your soul." Making moral decisions that have to do with sexual desires often does not come easily. In no area of life has Christianity meant more to the civilizing process than in the area of moral conduct. Christianity has steadfastly spoken out against sexual immorality without destroying the drive to live, to enjoy, and to experience.

Other major religions like Hinduism, Buddhism, Mohammedanism, and even Roman Catholicism have made asceticism and withdrawal from this world the highest form of godliness.

Christianity has stated boldly that the highest form of faith is evidenced in the life of the Christ who refused to isolate Himself from the worst and lowest levels of society. The power of a Christ-centered life is not demonstrated in withdrawal, but in godly choices made in the face of evil. The fact that our society has caved in to pressure to accept as "normal" homosexuality, pornography, abortion, greed, jealousy, corruption, premarital and extramarital sex, and divorce has placed great obligation on the Christian community to speak clearly and consistently in opposition.

It is not enough for Christians to be internally opposed to immorality, while adopting an external politically-correct posture. Evil triumphs when God's people are silent. We must remember that just because a moral issue is socially acceptable does mean that it is spiritually acceptable. The Christian community must speak out and our voice must be clear and consistent. Not only must we *speak* clearly and consistently, we must also live clearly and consistently. And we need to remember that overeating, gossip, and materialism are all spiritual and moral issues.

Peter says that these sinful desires wage "war against [the] soul" (1 Peter 2:11). Immorality eats at and eventually destroys the most God-like thing about us, the very thing that raises us above the animal level—our souls.

The soul and the conscience are closely related. When the soul is negated, we lose the only human quality that brings a sense of guilt and shame and elevates human behavior in the direction of what it means to be civilized. Paul writes in 1 Corinthians 6:9-11: "Do you not know that the wicked will not inherit the kingdom of God? Do not be deceived: Neither the sexually immoral nor idolaters nor adulterers nor male prostitutes nor homosexual offenders nor thieves nor the greedy nor drunkards nor slanderers nor swindlers will inherit the kingdom of God. And that is what some of you were. But you were washed, you were sanctified, you were *justified* in the name of the Lord Jesus Christ and by the Spirit of our God."

Paul says that our moral conduct is part of our testimony to the world that the Christ has changed us.

Questions for 1 Peter 2:11, 12

1. Because we are a holy nation and a royal priesthood, what are we also called?

2. Christians see life not as an end but as what?

3. How is a Christian's view of the world similar to an iceberg?

4. Discuss this statement: "The power of a Christ-centered life is not demonstrated in withdrawal, but in godly choices made in the face of evil."

5. Do you agree with this statement? "It is not enough for Christians to be *internally* opposed to immorality, while adopting an *external* politically-correct posture."

6. What does Peter mean when he says that sinful desires wage "war against [the] soul"?

Submit yourselves for the Lord's sake to every authority instituted among men: whether to the king, as the supreme authority, or to governors, who are sent by him to punish those who do wrong and to commend those who do right. For it is God's will that by doing good you should silence the ignorant talk of foolish men. Live as free men, but do not use your freedom as a cover-up for evil; live as servants of God. Show proper respect to everyone: Love the brotherhood of believers, fear God, honor the king (1 Peter 2:13-17).

Submission is the result of humility. It is the antithesis of pride and self-centeredness. Peter deals with the principle of submission in four specific areas:

1. Submission of all Christians to government (1 Peter 2:13-17)
2. Submission of Christian slaves to their masters (2:18-20)
3. Submission of Christian wives to their husbands (3:1-6)
4. Submission of Christian husbands to God (2:16; 3:7)

Paul writes in Romans 13:1-2, 7: "Everyone must submit himself to the governing authorities, for there is no authority except that which God has established. The authorities that exist have been established by God. Consequently, he who rebels against the authority is rebelling against what God has instituted, and those who do so will bring judgment on themselves...Give everyone what you owe him: If you owe taxes, pay taxes; if revenue, then revenue; if respect, then respect; if honor, then honor."

Paul says that Christians must submit to all human governmental institutions—to kings, presidents, and governors. We must be subject not only when we agree with them, but also when we disagree. The principle of a slave being obedient to an overbearing master has important implications for every submission situation.

Why do we submit? Peter says we submit to others as a sign of our submission to God and to silence unbelievers. Why should unbelievers ridicule us?

Are there exceptions? Of course there are. When Christians are faced with a situation in which to obey the legal authorities means to disobey God, they obey God. That principle is spelled out in the refusal of

Shadrach, Meshach, and Abednego to bow down to Nebuchadnezzar's idol (Daniel 3). But we must be very careful not to use the exceptions to justify bad behavior.

The key to submission in all circumstances is humility. Paul tells us in Philippians 2:1-8 that humility is essential to harmony, peace, joy, love, and unity. In spite of this attitude of submission, we are to "live as free men." That means that our submission is *a* voluntary one. We *choose* to submit. If we are forced to submit, there is no testimony for the gospel.

Christ has set us free! We submit not as mindless slaves, but as liberated thinkers, because our own will has been voluntarily bent to the will of God. We submit out of love for God and our desire to please Him. But we refuse to use our Christian freedom as an excuse to further our own ends (Matthew 17:24-27).

Questions for 1 Peter 2:13-17

1. Peter deals with the principle of submission in what four specific areas?
2. The principle of a slave being obedient to an overbearing master has what important implications for every submission situation?
3. What possible exceptions are there to the submission principle?
4. What should our attitude toward submission be?

Slaves, submit yourselves to your masters with all respect, not only to those who are good and considerate, but also to those who are harsh. For it is commendable if a man bears up under the pain of unjust suffering because he is conscious of God. But how is it to your credit if you receive a beating for doing wrong and endure it? But if you suffer for doing good and you endure it, this is commendable before God. To this you were called, because Christ suffered for you, leaving you an example, that you should follow in his steps (1 Peter 2:18-21).

Peter gives some specific instructions to Christian slaves. They are to submit to their masters voluntarily. As Americans we cringe at the thought of human bondage and wonder why God should view it with such apparent unconcern. It is very hard for us to see the world through God's eyes. I would suggest that God has very few "social concerns." God is primarily concerned with one thing only—our salvation.

The Bible is filled with evidence that leads us to understand that what happens to us between birth and death is only important to God as it relates to our salvation. The reason for this instruction to slaves is further proof of where God's concern lies. Slaves are to submit to their masters with respect in order to model the attitude of their Savior, the Christ who submitted Himself to Pilate and to the Jews in order to find favor with God.

The book of Philemon and its story of Paul's plea on behalf of Onesimus is a wonderful example of how Christians are to submit and relate to each other. Slaves are to submit with respect for the position the owner has and for the sake of their testimony to the power there is in a Christ-centered life. If Christian slaves only submit to good masters, then Christian slaves are no better than non-Christian ones.

Questions for 1 Peter 2:18-21

1. How are slaves to submit to their masters?
2. Why is it so hard for us to see the world through God's eyes?
3. God is only concerned with what one thing as it related to us?

"He committed no sin, and no deceit was found in his mouth." When they hurled their insults at him, he did not retaliate; when he suffered, he made no threats. Instead, he entrusted himself to him who judges justly. He himself bore our sins in his body on the tree, so that we might die to sins and live for righteousness; by his wounds you have been healed. For you were like sheep going astray, but now you have returned to the Shepherd and Overseer of your souls (1 Peter 2:22-25).

Christ is our example. He submitted *voluntarily.* In John 10:17, 18 Jesus gives this explanation to His disciples for His willingness to submit to the demands for His death: "The reason my Father loves me is that I lay down my life—only to take it up again. No one takes it from me, but I lay it down of my own accord. I have authority to lay it down and authority to take it up again. This command I received from my Father."

The power of Christianity is seen in the willingness of its adherents to submit—to choose submission as those who have been freed from the bondage of self-service. Before the gospel came, the people Peter is writing to were living like sheep, totally enslaved to the wishes of whatever shepherd owned them. They were in absolute bondage to sin, to themselves, and to those who ruled over them. When they obeyed the gospel, they were freed from the tyranny of involuntary service to sin, of service to government, and of service to self. All of their choices were restored to them.

Questions for 1 Peter 2:22-25

1. What explanation does Jesus gives to His disciples for His willingness to submit to the demands for His death?
2. How is the power of Christianity seen?
3. How does Christianity restore all of our choices?

FIRST PETER
CHAPTER 3

Wives, in the same way be submissive to your husbands so that, if any of them do not believe the word, they may be won over without words by the behavior of their wives, when they see the purity and reverence of your lives. Your beauty should not come from outward adornment, such as braided hair and the wearing of gold jewelry and fine clothes. Instead, it should be that of your inner self, the unfading beauty of a gentle and quiet spirit, which is of great worth in God's sight. For this is the way the holy women of the past who put their hope in God used to make themselves beautiful. They were submissive to their own husbands, like Sarah, who obeyed Abraham and called him her master. You are her daughters if you do what is right and do not give way to fear (1 Peter 3:1-6).

Part 1
We need to give Peter and the Holy Spirit credit for tackling what has always been a difficult problem—the principle of submission, especially as it relates to husband and wife relationships. It was a problem in the first century, and it is a problem now. At some point, virtually every marriage is confronted with an issue that raises the "who is in control" question. Very rarely is the issue ever resolved. It continues to crop up periodically because the root causes are never addressed. Give careful consideration to the following questions:

1. How many of you who are reading or studying this book were really looking forward to the discussion of these verses?

2. How many of you were a little nervous about what might be said?

3. More importantly, how many were defensive and had your guard up because you feared what was coming?

4. How many were hoping that what I might say would change the behavior or attitude of your mate?

It is interesting that the current cultural mindset with which we approach these verses is almost always negative. We don't like these verses! Women especially may be predisposed to insult, even anger, at what seems to them to be unfair, chauvinistic, Neanderthal, and demeaning statements that are calculated to keep them in their place.

It is important to remember that everything God has told us is for our good and it is critical that we approach every biblical teaching with that mindset. God intended for the marriage relationship to bring peace, harmony, and joy to our lives. It was not intended to be adversarial in nature. Listen to what Peter says in 1 Peter 3:8, 9: "Finally, all of you, live in harmony with one another; be sympathetic, love as brothers, be compassionate and humble. Do not repay evil with evil or insult with insult, but with blessing, because to this you were called so that you may inherit a blessing."

Peter says that Christians were called by God so that they might inherit the blessings of peace and harmony. The attitude with which we approach these verses on submission will determine whether or not we are blessed with peace and harmony. If the men say, "I'm so glad we're studying these verses because my wife really needs to hear them," that is the wrong attitude. If the wives say, "I just can't wait until we get to 1 Peter 3:7. My husband really needs to listen to it!" That is the wrong attitude. If our focus is on how these verses need to impact the person we're married to, we will never be molded into the image of the risen Christ.

If we approach a passage negatively, it is an indication that we are convicted by it. If we excuse our disobedience on the basis of the failure of our mates or others to obey passages that apply to them, that is self-defeating. How other people respond to the teachings of Scripture must not be the standard by which we decide if we are going to be obedient to what applies to us. We all need to have the attitude of embracing every passage that applies to us, not on focusing on passages that we can apply to others.

The question I always encounter when teaching on this topic is, "But what if I submit and the person I'm married to takes advantage of me?" That is a legitimate question and unfortunately, a very real possibility.

My first response is that our obedience to God must never be based on the obedience of others. Disobedience on the part of others does not excuse our disobedience. I think Peter gives us part of the answer in 1 Peter 5:7 when he says, "Cast all of your anxiety on him because he cares for you." When our obedience to God causes us pain we must cast our cares on Him.

Another important part of the answer is in 1 Peter 5:5: "[God] gives grace to the humble." He will lift up the humble "in due [or at the proper] time" (v. 6). If we refuse to humble ourselves and submit according to God's instructions, it is because of our pride.

The principle of submission is a continuous thread that runs the entire length of the New Testament. The foundation upon which this sometimes tedious, sometimes onerous instruction rests is simply and completely the example of Jesus. Humility is the key to all submission. First Peter 5:5 says: "All of you, clothe yourselves with humility toward one another, because, 'God opposes the proud but gives grace to the humble.' "

What is easily overlooked in these passages is that Peter addresses his submission instructions to those very classes of people who had absolutely no choices at all in their culture—slaves, women, and common citizens. Because they had no legal or moral rights, they were already in submission.

The irony is that in the culture of the first century, it was the slave owners, governing authorities, and husbands who had the most reason to be put off, upset by, and to dislike and rebel against these teachings. They were the ones who were going to have to give up the most, change the most, and humble themselves the most.

What makes these passages fascinating is that Peter makes choosers out of people who legally and socially had no choices. He admonishes them to choose to submit. The basis for his remarks is that their response to the gospel has gained for them the freedom of choice that is in Christ. Having the power to choose to submit changes everything.

Paul reinforces Peter's instruction in 1 Corinthians 7:21, 22 when he says: "Were you a slave when you were called? Don't let it trouble you—although if you can gain your freedom, do so. For he who was a slave when he was called by the Lord is the Lord's freedman; similarly, he who was a free man when he was called is Christ's slave."

The submission that Peter is talking about is based on making a choice to submit. Christian submission is not based on force or inferiority but on having the mind of Christ. These biblical principles relate directly, not only to the topic of husband-wife relationships but also to submission in *all* Christian relationships. How do we know that these are principles and not specific commands? Because Peter gives us no examples of how this works or makes specific applications. For instance, in 1 Peter 2:17 Peter says: "Show proper respect to everyone." We could ask several legitimate questions about this injunction.

1. First, what is "respect"?
2. Second, what is *"proper"*?
3. Third, who does "everyone" include?

The Holy Spirit says, "You figure it out." We are left to our own spiritual discernment as to how to apply these principles. Submission in any relationship is based on humility, as evidenced by the example of the submission of Jesus to the Jews and Romans. That is why Peter keeps saying "in the same way" (1 Peter 3:1, 7; 5:5).

In 1 Peter 2:18, slaves are to submit to their masters. In 3:1, wives are to submit to their husbands. In verse 3:7, husbands are to submit to Christ. In verse 3:8, all Christians are enjoined to "live in harmony" and be "compassionate and humble."

How did Jesus demonstrate His submission? What example did the Christ leave us? Jesus didn't just *talk* about humility and submission, He *did* it. Paul instructs the Christians at Philippi in Philippians 2:5-8 as follows: "Your attitude should be the same as that of Christ Jesus: Who, being in very nature God, did not consider equality with God something to be grasped, but made himself nothing, taking the very nature of a servant, being made in human likeness. And being found in appearance as a man, he humbled himself and became obedient to death—even death on a cross!"

The Christ made Himself nothing. It was a decision! He not only decided but he acted by taking the form of a servant. He humbled Himself. He was obedient. That is the result of humility.

John tells us the extent to which Jesus went to demonstrate His humility in John 13:3-5, 12-16:

Jesus knew that the Father had put all things under his power, and that he had come from God and was returning to God; so he got up from the meal, took off his outer clothing, and wrapped a towel around his waist. After that, he poured water into a basin and began to wash his disciples' feet, drying them with the towel that was wrapped around him...When he had finished washing their feet, he put on his clothes and returned to his place. "Do you understand what I have done for you?" he asked them. "You call me 'Teacher' and 'Lord,' and rightly so, for that is what I am. Now that I, your Lord and Teacher, have washed your feet, you also should wash one another's feet. I have set you an example that you should do as I have done for you. I tell you the truth, no servant is greater than his master, nor is a messenger greater than the one who sent him."

The Christ not only denied Himself on the cross, He denied Himself on a daily basis in His life. He was servant of all and taught His disciples that they were not to be called "Rabbi" or "Master" (Matthew 23:8). Self-denial befits a Christian because it typifies the Lord we serve. Self-denial saves us from self-indulgence.

In 1 Peter 2:13 Peter admonishes all Christians to "[s]ubmit yourselves for the Lord's sake to every authority instituted among men." Submitting ourselves is a choice. In verses 21, 22 he gives the foundation for all Christian humility and submission: "To this you were called, because Christ suffered for you, leaving you an example, that you should follow in his steps. 'He committed no sin, and no deceit was found in his mouth.'"

Here we find the answer to what "in the same way" means. It means

1. in the same way that Jesus submitted to unjust people.
2. in the same way that Jesus bore our sins on the cross in submission to God.
3. in that same way slaves are to be in submission to their masters, wives are to be in submission to their husbands, and all Christians are to be in submission to governing authorities and to each other.
4. all of this submission is based on the example left to us by the Christ, "that [we] should follow in his steps" (1 Peter 2:21).

Reread 1 Peter 3:1, 2: "Wives, in the same way be submissive to your husbands so that, if any of them do not believe the word, they may be won over without words by the behavior of their wives, when they see the purity and reverence of your lives."

Peter first states the general principle of submission of wives to their husbands. He then applies the principle to a specific situation—women whose husbands are not Christians. Remember that most of the Christians at this time became Christians as adults. That means that there were very few second-generation Christians; so the problems that are generated when one mate becomes a Christian and the other does not must have been pretty common.

Peter says that Christian wives should submit to non-Christian husbands "in the same way" that Jesus submitted. In 1 Peter 3:6 Peter even urges wives to be "like Sarah, who obeyed Abraham and called him her master." (Please note that I only mention this because the Holy Spirit said it. I am in no way recommending or even suggesting that current husbands push this point.)

Peter says that Sarah called Abraham "master." What is unfortunate for us is that cultural circumstances have conspired to make the kind of submissive attitude that is represented by the word "master" repugnant to most women. It isn't the word that's important—it's the attitude.

Questions for 1 Peter 3:1-6 (Part 1)

1. Submission was a problem in the first century, and it is a problem now. Why?

2. Why is the "control issue" rarely ever resolved?

3. Do you believe that God intended for the marriage relationship to bring peace, harmony, and joy to our lives?

4. What kind of mindset do we need to approach these verses?

5. How do we answer the question: "But what if I submit and the person I'm married to takes advantage of me?"

6. What classes of people does Peter address his submission comments to? Why is that important?

7. How do we know that these are "principles" and not "commands"? What is the difference?

8. How did Jesus demonstrate His submission? What example did He leave us?

9. What principle is Christian submission based upon?

Wives, in the same way be submissive to your husbands so that, if any of them do not believe the word, they may be won over without words by the behavior of their wives, when they see the purity and reverence of your lives. Your beauty should not come from outward adornment, such as braided hair and the wearing of gold jewelry and fine clothes. Instead, it should be that of your inner self, the unfading beauty of a gentle and quiet spirit, which is of great worth in God's sight. For this is the way the holy women of the past who put their hope in God used to make themselves beautiful. They were submissive to their own husbands, like Sarah, who obeyed Abraham and called him her master. You are her daughters if you do what is right and do not give way to fear (1 Peter 3:1-6).

Part 2

Peter says that unbelieving husbands may be won to the gospel by their wives' humble and submissive behavior rather than their *words*. Paul says basically the same thing in 1 Corinthians 7. This attitude of submission should be evidenced by Christian women in practical ways. It should be reflected in the way they dress and the kind of ornamentation they adorn themselves with. The outer appearance of Christian women should be a reflection of their commitment to Christ and to their marriage.

The following story is attributed to President Abraham Lincoln. A lady came to visit him one day. When she left his office Lincoln remarked to his secretary, "That was a well-dressed woman." The secretary said, "I didn't even notice what she had on." Lincoln said, "Neither did I. That's how I know she was well dressed."

What does Peter mean by "behavior" in 1 Peter 3:1, 2? He means that there must be purity and reverence in the lives of all Christians. Purity refers to moral attitudes, and reverence refers to godliness.

In 2004, Christian pollster, George Barna polled hundreds of Christians with a questionnaire asking if they ever had extra-marital affairs, if they were involved in any kind of pornography, if they ever cheated on their income tax, if they watched R-rated movies, if they used foul language, if they drank alcoholic beverages, etc.

Then Barna gave the same questionnaire to the same number of people who professed no faith at all. When he got all of his statistics compiled, guess what he learned? There was no difference between people who go to church and those who don't when it comes to the practical impact of Christianity.

In 2 Corinthians 7:1 Paul says: "Since we have these promises, dear friends, let us purify ourselves from everything that contaminates body and spirit, perfecting holiness out of reverence for God."

Paul challenges Christians with a lifestyle—a way of deciding value—that is so advanced, so otherworldly, so far above the level at which we actually live, that I fear we do not take it seriously and therefore make little attempt to put it into practice. The purification that Paul speaks of here is a deliberate choice that we make. It is a choice that eliminates all other possible lifestyles. It is a choice that influences every aspect of our lives.

Paul says that what motivate us to make a choice like that are the "promises" God has made to those who make that choice (2 Corinthians 7:1). What are those promises? If we look for them in the preceding verses, we will find those very disturbing—almost embarrassing—words of 6:14-18,

> Do not be yoked together with unbelievers. For what do righteousness and wickedness have in common? Or what fellowship can light have with darkness? What harmony is there between Christ and Belial? What does a believer have in common with an unbeliever? What agreement is there between the temple of God and idols? For we are the temple of the living God. As God has said: 'I will live with them and walk among them, and I will be their God, and they will be my people.' 'Therefore come out from them and be separate, says the Lord. Touch no unclean thing, and I will receive you. I will be a Father to you, and you will be my sons and daughters, says the Lord Almighty.'

The promises are
1. that we are the temple of the living God;
2. that God will live with us, and walk among us;
3. that He will be our personal God;
4. that He will be a Father to us by acknowledging us as His sons and daughters.

Those are awesome promises—incredible, unbelievable promises—but like purity, they are conditional. The conditions are part of the purifying process, which is
1. not being yoked with unbelievers;
2. being separate from the world;

3. touching no unclean things;

4. purifying ourselves from everything that contaminates;

5. perfecting holiness out of reverence for God.

How do we "purify ourselves from everything that contaminates" (2 Corinthians 7:1)? The area that Peter addresses is one of the least obvious and most difficult to talk about. It is modesty. How do we teach modesty to our children? We have learned that we can't legislate it. We must model it! Modesty is a moral principle. It is not a legal requirement. The problem with principles is that they force us to think—and to think spiritually. We are most uncomfortable when we have to think about something rather than just blindly obeying. It is possible to obey laws physically and have a heart of disobedience. It isn't possible to do that with principles because there is no requirement for obeying principles. A good heart is the only requirement.

With principles like modesty we must first *want* to obey; that isn't easy, because we live in a culture that constantly encourages immodesty. We watch movies, TV shows, and videos—even commercials—that mold our minds to accept a dress code that is totally out of harmony with the principle of modesty. The truth is that for all practical purposes we have given up. We don't even talk about modesty anymore. One of the reasons for that is because modesty hasn't been legally defined, we feel powerless to teach authoritatively about what it is and when it is being violated.

What Paul writes in 1 Timothy 2: 9, 10, "I also want women to dress modestly, with decency and propriety, not with braided hair, or gold, or pearls or expensive clothes, but with good deeds, appropriate for women who profess to worship God," is very similar to Peter's words in 1 Peter 3:1-4. If we approach this passage with an attitude of determining everything that it doesn't mean by writing it off as cultural, we are saying that it doesn't mean anything—and the Holy Spirit was wasting His time.

What is it that makes us want to dress immodestly or at least look at those who do? Let's get real here. It is the sinful nature. It is the flesh. We must be more honest with our motives in how we dress. I was forcefully reminded of this at a congregation I used to preach for. We held a banquet our teenagers called "True Love Waits." It did me a great deal of good to hear a young lady talk honestly about how she overcomes her "want to" in this area. She said that she is aware that she has a good figure. She said that she knows that the way she dresses makes a statement to the boys about who she is and about where her head is in regard to sex.

I hear so many people say that they aren't responsible for what other people think; but that's a lie, and we know it. There has never been a more clothes-conscious culture in the history of the world. The truth is that everybody dresses in a way to make a statement about themselves. It was refreshing to hear this young lady say that she believes that *she* is responsible for what boys think when they see her. She said that she looks in the mirror every morning before she leaves the house and asks herself what the guys are going to think when they look at her. She also asks herself what *she* thinks when she looks at herself. For that reason she doesn't wear tight-fitting clothes, and she doesn't wear necklines that display too much.

I suspect that every person asks the same questions for different reasons. You may not have noticed but people don't put earrings in their behinds and they don't put tattoos under their armpits or on the soles of their feet. They put them where others can see them. Why? Give me a break—because they make a statement about the person who has them.

What kinds of sexual messages do we send with the way we dress? Do we dress deliberately to display our devotion to God? Or do we dress to show our conformity to this world? In reference to your dress, the movies you watch, the places you go, the jokes you tell, the topics that dominate your conversation—are you purifying yourself from everything that might contaminate your body and spirit? Are you "perfecting holiness out of reverence for God" (2 Corinthians 7:1)? Are you thinking spiritually?

You can't read wrong, watch wrong, listen wrong—and think right!

Returning to our topic of submission, are there parameters around the principle of submission? Of course there are. If a woman, or an employee, or a citizen asks, "Do you mean that I just have to take it when my husband abuses me, or when my boss tells me to do something that is unethical, or if my government asks me to act contrary to my conscience?" Those are legitimate questions, and they demand an answer.

Although there are no ironclad, legalistic answers to questions like that, we do have biblical principles that might govern us. There are principles like: "We must obey God rather than men!" (Acts 5:29), and like the response of the apostles when they were told by the constituted government to stop preaching about Jesus (4:19, 20). There are also working-out-your-own-salvation principles that would apply to destructive, severely abusive situations. There is a huge difference between submission and masochism.

What further complicates issues like this is that there are all kinds and definitions of what is destructive, unbearable, and abusive. Sometimes, the answer to the question, "Do I have to take it?" might be, "Yes, you have to take it, because that is what Jesus did." Sometimes the answer might be "No, because it would violate God's will for my life."

Deciding requires a great deal of prayer, introspection, study, and especially spiritual discernment, rather than cultural definition. The wife's submission is not based on fear of her husband or what he might do. It is based on a choice to humble herself and submit to God. The question I asked earlier: "But what if I submit and he takes advantage of it?" is a legitimate question, and that is exactly what has produced the tension. The answer comes from Peter's admonition to men, which will be noted later.

It is good to remember that Peter's instructions were intended exclusively for the Christian community—not for the general population. God's instructions for marital relationships only work properly when both husband and wife are in submission to Him. It is also important for us to remember that in 2 Corinthians 6:14-18 God gives specific instructions that *His* people must marry *His* people. When we deliberately violate His will for our lives, chaos, sin, and adversarial relationships can result.

What is Peter's point? He is not concerned with rights but with testimony. He is not concerned with who is in charge or who is boss. He is concerned with God's will and our salvation. He specifically points out that the wife's submission to her unbelieving husband is so that "they may be won" (1 Peter 3:1). If God had designed the family with the wife as leader, Peter would have urged submission of the husband just as sincerely and for the same purpose.

All self-denial, humility, and submission begin with the submission that is based on humility before God. First Peter 5:6: "Humble yourselves, therefore, under God's mighty hand, that he may lift you up in due time." Mark 8:34, 35: "Then he called the crowd to him along with his disciples and said: 'If anyone would come after me, he must deny himself and take up his cross and follow me. For whoever wants to save his life will lose it, but whoever loses his life for me and for the gospel will save it.'"

What are the characteristics of a person who is trying to save his or her life? What does that mean? Trying to save your life means that you are focused on this world and yourself. It means that your conversation is sprinkled with words like: *"I'm* tired!" *"I* don't feel good." *"I* need." *"I'm* hungry." *"I'm* uncomfortable." *"I* don't like that." "Nobody has called or come to see *me."*

Trying to lose your life for Jesus means that you are focused on others. Your conversation is sprinkled with words like: *"You* must be tired." *"You* must not feel good." *"You* must need." *"You* must be hungry." "I'm sure *you* don't like that." *"I* must call and go to see this person today."

We humble ourselves in our human relationships because we have humbled ourselves before God. Humility leads to obedience. James 3:13: "Who is wise and understanding among you? Let him show it by his good life, by deeds done in the humility that comes from wisdom." The principles of turning the other cheek, going the extra mile, and giving up your cloak and coat are acts of obedience to God based on our willingness to submit to His directions.

This is the same argument Peter makes in 1 Peter 2:13, 18 to all Christians: Christ is our example. If a wife's reaction to this is, "I don't care what it says, no man is going tell me what to do," she does not have the Spirit of Christ. If a husband's reaction is, "I don't care what it says, no woman is going to run my life," he does not have the Spirit of Christ.

Questions for 1 Peter 3:1-6 (Part 2)

1. What "principle" is involved in Peter's comments on how women dress?

2. Discuss this statement: "The outer appearance of Christian women should be a reflection of their commitment to Christ and to their marriage."

3. What does this statement mean to you? "You can't read wrong, watch wrong, listen wrong—and think right"!

4. From what we read in 2 Corinthians 7, how do we "purify ourselves from everything that contaminates" (v. 1)?

5. What makes us want to dress immodestly or at least look at those who do?

6. What is being gratified by your appearance?

7. What is appropriate dress? What statement does your appearance make?

8. Do we dress deliberately to display our devotion to God? Or do we dress to show our conformity to this world?

9. What do braided hair, gold jewelry, and fine clothes translate into today?

10. Would you ladies say that you have a "gentle and quiet spirit"? Do you "want" to have one? Would you husbands agree with that?

11. The promises of God are based on what conditions?

12. Are we responsible for what other people think?

13. Are there parameters around the principle of submission? What biblical principles might guide us as we deal with that question?

14. Discuss this statement: "God's instructions for marital relationships only work properly when both husband and wife are in submission to Him."

15. Do you believe that it is a sin for a Christian to marry a non-Christian? Why?

Husbands, in the same way be considerate as you live with your wives, and treat them with respect as the weaker partner and as heirs with you of the gracious gift of life, so that nothing will hinder your prayers (1 Peter 3:7).

"[I]n the same way" as what? Again, in the same way that Christ left us an example that we should follow in His footsteps, husbands are to follow the example of Jesus in their relationships with their wives. The words "in the same way" imply that there is a sense in which husbands are to have an attitude of submission to their wives. Just as Christ was submissive to government and to circumstances when He had the right to refuse, so husbands must have humility—not arrogance—in dealing with their wives. They must look *first* to themselves.

What does Peter mean by the "weaker partner" (1 Peter 3:7)? The "partner" aspect of the injunction is easily overlooked and nearly always underemphasized. It speaks to a relationship based on spiritual equality. The tendency to focus on "weaker" has made this passage even more repugnant to women than I believe Peter intended. In fact, I believe that the Holy Spirit intended this passage to give balance to the previous instruction. If the wife is primarily viewed by the husband as his partner, the passage only indicates what most of us already admit—that generally speaking, women "break" more easily and that God created them to be more fragile in both physical and emotional construction. But that "weakness" is the very thing that gives balance to the relationship because it makes women more tender, sensitive, compassionate, and creative in emotional and aesthetic areas.

I believe also that "weaker partner" refers to the wife's vulnerability because of God's instruction to be submissive to her husband. Husbands are instructed not to take advantage of or abuse their headship role. God will deal severely with those who abuse their power. Eve was taken out of Adam and created by God with the specific intent of being Adam's "helper" (Genesis 2:18). "Helper" is not a degrading term; it is a designation of purpose. Husbands are to treat their wives with honor. They do that not out of condescension but because they accept her as a partner and fellow "heir" of grace. That means that both husband and wife are equally living under grace. That means that the wife is equal to the husband in value to God and in the kingdom.

Peter urges consideration in husbands. It is a key term that means to be understanding and sensitive toward her needs. When husbands are understanding and sensitive, wives find it much easier to be submissive. That is the way it was supposed to work, and it was intended to bring joy and peace to the marriage relationship. When our pride and fear causes us to fight against God's design, discord and unhappiness are the result.

If a Christian wife asks, "Do I have to be submissive to a husband who does not treat me as a partner and who is not understanding, sensitive, and considerate?"—or when a Christian husband asks, "Do I have to be understanding, sensitive, and considerate to a wife who is not submissive?"—we need to look just a few verses down in this same chapter. In 1 Peter 3:8, 9 Peter says: "Finally, all of you, live in harmony with one another; [all of you] be sympathetic, [all of you] love as brothers, [all of you] be compassionate and humble. [all of you] Do not repay evil with evil or insult with insult, but with blessing, because to this [all of you] were called so that [all of you] may inherit a blessing." Peter says that when some do not act in harmony with God's instructions, it only increases the obligation of those around them.

Questions for 1 Peter 3:7

1. Discuss what you think it means that the words "in the same way" imply that there is a sense in which husbands are to have an attitude of submission to their wives.
2. What does Peter mean by the "weaker partner"?
3. What does it mean that husbands should be "considerate" toward their wives?

Finally, all of you, live in harmony with one another; be sympathetic, love as brothers, be compassionate and humble. Do not repay evil with evil or insult with insult, but with blessing, because to this you were called so that you may inherit a blessing. For, "Whoever would love life and see good days must keep his tongue from evil and his lips from deceitful speech. He must turn from evil and do good; he must seek peace and pursue it. For the eyes of the Lord are on the righteous and his ears are attentive to their prayer, but the face of the Lord is against those who do evil" (1 Peter 3:8-12).

"Finally" indicates a summation of the submission section. God wants all of His children to live in harmony. All Christians are to be sympathetic, brotherly, kind, and humble in spirit in all of their relationships. If that means doing the dirty jobs, we should do them and do them willingly. Being treated badly does not justify treating others badly. Bad behavior cannot be justified; it can only be repented of. We must want peace, and we must act in such a way that peace is promoted. When we react to bad behavior by yelling, cursing, name calling and then justify our bad behavior on the basis of what others are doing, it is a violation of God's will for our lives. It is a sin.

God is the author of right relationships. Until we are rightly related to God we can never be rightly related to anyone else. God created marriage to be peaceful and harmonious. When there are relational problems, somebody is sinning. When we act out of harmony with the submission and consideration principles, not only does our marriage relationship suffer, our relationship with God suffers; and He does not hear our prayers. Isaiah warns us in Isaiah 59:1, 2: "Surely the arm of the LORD is not too short to save, nor his ear too dull to hear. But your iniquities have separated you from your God; your sins have hidden his face from you, so that he will not hear."

Questions for 1 Peter 3:8-12

1. God wants all His children to live in harmony. What are steps we can take to live in harmony with Christian brothers and sisters who stir up conflict, who are difficult to deal with, who put us in difficult situations, etc.?

2. Discuss this statement: "Being treated badly does not justify treating others badly."

3. Do you believe that until we are rightly related to God we can never be rightly related to anyone else?

4. In what ways can Christian men and women make their marriages more peaceful and harmonious?

Who is going to harm you if you are eager to do good? But even if you should suffer for what is right, you are blessed. "Do not fear what they fear; do not be frightened." But in your hearts set apart Christ as Lord. Always be prepared to give an answer to everyone who asks you to give the reason for the hope that you have. But do this with gentleness and respect, keeping a clear conscience, so that those who speak maliciously against your good behavior in Christ may be ashamed of their slander. It is better, if it is God's will, to suffer for doing good than for doing evil (1 Peter 3:13-17).

God protects those who "do good." What does He protect us from? Not from persecution. Not from suffering or harm but from more than we can bear. Consider the following passages:

1. Romans 5:3-5: "Not only so, but we also rejoice in our sufferings, because we know that suffering produces perseverance; perseverance, character; and character, hope. And hope does not disappoint us, because God has poured out his love into our hearts by the Holy Spirit, whom he has given us."

2. Romans 8:17, 18: "Now if we are children, then we are heirs—heirs of God and co-heirs with Christ, if indeed we share in his sufferings in order that we may also share in his glory. I consider that our present sufferings are not worth comparing with the glory that will be revealed in us."

3. 2 Corinthians 1:5-7: "For just as the sufferings of Christ flow over into our lives, so also through Christ our comfort overflows. If we are distressed, it is for your comfort and salvation; if we are comforted, it is for your comfort, which produces in you patient endurance of the same sufferings we suffer. And our hope for you is firm, because we know that just as you share in our sufferings, so also you share in our comfort."

Suffering for doing what is right brings a blessing. That blessing is the satisfaction we feel when we are considered "worthy" of participating in the sufferings of Christ and bear "in our own bodies" His shame and humiliation.

First Peter 3:14: "Do not fear what they fear; do not be frightened." We are often intimidated by those about us. We call it "peer pressure." When someone says, "You mean you don't have one of these?" or "You mean you haven't seen that movie?" or "So do you think you're better than me because you don't drink, gamble, go to bars, or watch certain movies?"—that is intimidation! We tend to modify our behavior to prohibit ridicule or disapproval.

Attitudes expressed, entertainment participated in, political ideas advocated, material read, things disapproved, and what is laughed at are all often group decisions rather than personal ones. Peter basically says, "Don't be troubled, downcast and feel rejected when you don't fit in." Christians aren't supposed to fit in. In fact, fitting in is a warning to us that we are failing in our commitment to God and to the gospel. Having the mind of Christ guarantees that we are going to be pilgrims and strangers.

First Peter 3:15: To "set apart Christ as Lord" means that we make Jesus not just the Savior of our souls but the Lord of our lives. Peter essentially says, "Always be ready to jump at the chance to testify about your faith, your conduct, and your goals, and to explain why you're different; but do it with gentleness and reverence, not with arrogance, or condescension." In verse 16 Peter says that we should keep a "clear conscience." That means that we must not lie to ourselves. A good conscience comes from knowing why we're doing what we're doing. It comes from a deliberate choice to be different. Verse 17 says: "[S]uffer for doing good than for doing evil." Everyone suffers in this world. Make sure you're suffering for the right reason.

Questions for 1 Peter 3:13-17

1. God protects those who "do good." What does He protect us from, and how does He do that?
2. Do you tend to modify your behavior to prohibit ridicule or disapproval?
3. "Christians aren't supposed to fit in." Do you agree or disagree with that statement? Why?
4. How do we develop a good conscience?
5. God wants all His children to live in harmony. What are steps we can take to live in harmony with Christian brothers and sisters who stir up conflict, who are difficult to deal with, who put us in difficult situations, etc.?

For Christ died for sins once for all, the righteous for the unrighteous, to bring you to God. He was put to death in the body but made alive by the Spirit, through whom also he went and preached to the spirits in prison who disobeyed long ago when God waited patiently in the days of Noah while the ark was being built. In it only a few people, eight in all, were saved through water, and this water symbolizes baptism that now saves you also—not the removal of dirt from the body but the pledge of a good conscience toward God. It saves you by the resurrection of Jesus Christ, who has gone into heaven and is at God's right hand—with angels, authorities and powers in submission to him (1 Peter 3:18-22).

Christ's death was "once for all" (1 Peter 3:18). What does that mean? Paul writes in Romans 6:8-11: "Now if we died with Christ, we believe that we will also live with him. For we know that since Christ was raised from the dead, he cannot die again; death no longer has mastery over him. The death he died, he died to sin once for all; but the life he lives, he lives to God. In the same way, count yourselves dead to sin but alive to God in Christ Jesus."

CHAPTER 3

Jesus' death on the cross was on behalf of the entire human race. There is no need for Him to die again because in His death He conquered death. Death no longer has power over Him because He is in His resurrected body which is imperishable.

The Hebrew writer explains it this way in Hebrews 2:14, 15: "Since the children have flesh and blood, he too shared in their humanity so that by his death he might destroy him who holds the power of death—that is, the devil—and free those who all their lives were held in slavery by their fear of death." Because of what Jesus did in His death and resurrection, we should fear death no longer.

Christ's death was "the righteous for the unrighteous" (1 Peter 3:18). When John the Baptist saw the Christ coming he said, "Look, the Lamb of God, who takes away the sins of the world!" (John 1:29). Peter says that Jesus' purpose in dying was to "bring [us] to God" (1 Peter 3:18).

Hebrews 7:22-27 says

> Because of this oath, Jesus has become the guarantee of a better covenant. Now there have been many of those priests, since death prevented them from continuing in office; but because Jesus lives forever, he has a permanent priesthood. Therefore he is able to save completely those who come to God through him, because he always lives to intercede for them. Such a high priest meets our need—one who is holy, blameless, pure, set apart from sinners, exalted above the heavens. Unlike the other high priests, he does not need to offer sacrifices day after day, first for his own sins, and then for the sins of the people. He sacrificed for their sins once for all when he offered himself.

Paul says, in Romans 6:11 that we should consider ourselves as "dead to sin" because of the death we died in baptism and "alive to God" because of the "new creation" (2 Corinthians 5:17) that God has performed by the power of the resurrection.

Christ died that (purpose) He might bring us to God. He was put to death in the flesh on the cross. How did He accomplish His purpose through His death? How does His death bring us to God? It is through His death and resurrection that we have the opportunity to experience the same death to sin and resurrection to a newly created life.

The power of the Holy Spirit to create spiritual life in us through the new birth was made possible through the death of Jesus. Spiritual life is animated by physical death. In 1 Corinthians 15:54-57 Paul explains it this way: "When the perishable has been clothed with the imperishable, and the mortal with immortality, then the saying that is written will come true: 'Death has been swallowed up in victory.' 'Where, O death, is your victory? Where, O death, is your sting?' The sting of death is sin, and the power of sin is the law. But thanks be to God! He gives us the victory through our Lord Jesus Christ."

And in Romans 7:24, 25 Paul says, "Who will rescue me from this body of death? Thanks be to God—through Jesus Christ our Lord!" The new birth brings us to God. It makes peace by removing the barrier between man and God—which is sin.

Peter says that when Jesus was put to death in the body, He was made alive in the spirit, and He went and preached to the spirits in prison (1 Peter 3:18, 19). This passage raises some questions. When did this occur? Where is this prison? Who was in this prison? Why were they there? What was the message? Was there any response?

When did Jesus do this preaching? I believe that it happened every time the prophets spoke by His Spirit. First Peter 1:10-12 says, "Concerning this salvation, the prophets, who spoke of the grace that was to come to you, searched intently and with the greatest care, trying to find out the time and circumstances to which the Spirit of Christ in them was pointing when he predicted the sufferings of Christ and the glories that would follow. It was revealed to them that they were not serving themselves but you, when they spoke of the things that have now been told you by those who have preached the gospel to you by the Holy Spirit sent from heaven. Even angels long to look into these things."

First Peter 4:6: "For this is the reason the gospel was preached even to those who are now dead, so that they might be judged according to men in regard to the body, but live according to God in regard to the spirit."

The preaching of the gospel that Peter refers to is not confined to post-Pentecostal preaching. Every prophetic call to repentance is a gospel message because it brings people to God through the sacrifice of Jesus.

What did Noah preach? Peter tells us in 2 Peter 2:5 that Noah was "a preacher of righteousness." He preached righteousness. He told the people to repent because God was going to send a flood on the earth. He told them that they were going to have to either accept God's salvation or perish. The purpose of all preaching is to convict people of sin and lead them to repentance.

To whom did Noah preach? Specifically, to those who are now in prison because of their disobedience to his preaching. But there is a very real sense in which Noah is still preaching to every person who hears the message of the flood.

Why were they in prison? Because they refused to listen. They perished because the message made no physical sense. Fleshly needs like heat, cold, hunger, thirst, and sleep consume our thoughts. Noah's preaching met stubborn resistance because all of the previous experiences of his audience prevented them from being able to imagine the flood. We need desperately to realize that the destruction of not only the earth—but the entire universe is just as surreal to people today as the flood was to the people of Noah's day. It is an interesting sidenote to realize that these people "in prison" have been in a state of conscious punishment since they died—and the judgment of God has not taken place yet.

Where is the prison? In the Hadean world—the same place where the rich man was in Luke 16 and also alluded to in Jude 6.

Eight persons were saved *through* water. We think of them as being saved *from* water. It is not so. The earth was doomed. Noah was saved *from* destruction by the water, which separated him from that destruction. The water set Noah apart from the rest of the world. The water brought death to the unbelieving and disobedient, and life to the believers and obedient.

Water still does the same thing. And that is why Peter says that "baptism . . . now saves" you (1 Peter 3:21) because baptism separates the saved from the lost and provides a separation between life and death. Baptism, the new birth, provides the means whereby we put off the dominion of the flesh by dying to it and initiate the dominion of the Spirit (Romans 6:1ff.).

Questions for 1 Peter 3:18-22

1. Peter says that Christ's death was "once for all" (1 Peter 3:18). What does that mean?

2. How did Jesus accomplish His purpose through His death?

3. How does His death bring us to God?

4. Peter says that when Jesus was put to death in the body but made alive in the spirit, He went and preached to the spirits in prison. This passage raises some questions. When did this occur?

5. Where is this prison?

6. Who was in this prison?

7. Why were they there?

8. What was the message?

9. Was there any response?

10. Peter says that Noah and family were saved "through" water. What does that mean?

11. Are we still saved through water today?

FIRST PETER
CHAPTER 4

Therefore, since Christ suffered in his body, arm yourselves also with the same attitude, because he who has suffered in his body is done with sin. As a result, he does not live the rest of his earthly life for evil human desires, but rather for the will of God. For you have spent enough time in the past doing what pagans choose to do—living in debauchery, lust, drunkenness, orgies, carousing and detestable idolatry. They think it strange that you do not plunge with them into the same flood of dissipation, and they heap abuse on you. But they will have to give account to him who is ready to judge the living and the dead. For this is the reason the gospel was preached even to those who are now dead, so that they might be judged according to men in regard to the body, but live according to God in regard to the spirit (1 Peter 4:1-6).

Part 1

Human beings have struggled from the beginning of time with the cause of suffering, especially those who believe in a loving, all-powerful, and just God who controls everything in the universe. Peter encourages the Christians to whom he writes to arm themselves with the attitude that the Christ had toward suffering.

The attitude that Jesus had when faced with the cross was not primarily one of concern about what He was going to suffer but whether His suffering would prevent Him from doing the will of God. That is the attitude that we need to arm ourselves with.

Many passages address suffering and our attitudes toward it in both the Old and New Testament. Some early Christians regarded suffering as a type of purifying or ennobling process. They also thought that if they suffered sufficiently, especially if their suffering led to death for Jesus' sake, it would guarantee they would go to heaven.

Hebrews 11:35 says: "Women received back their dead, raised to life again. Others were tortured and refused to be released, so that they might gain a better resurrection." The Roman church encouraged celibacy, fasting, total silence, even isolation and flagellation as methods of achieving spirituality and freedom from sin. Martin Luther wore a hair shirt and flagellated himself in an attempt to purify himself from fleshly lusts.

It is interesting that both Job and his friends regarded suffering as a sign that the sufferer had committed sin and that God was inflicting punishment for it. Eliphaz, in his speech to Job in 22:4-11, says

> "Is it for your piety that he rebukes you and brings charges against you? Is not your wickedness great? Are not your sins endless? You demanded security from your brothers for no reason; you stripped men of their clothing, leaving them naked. You gave no water to the weary and you withheld food from the hungry, though you were a powerful man, owning land—an honored man, living on it. And you sent widows away empty-handed and broke the strength of the fatherless. That is why snares are all around you, why sudden peril terrifies you, why it is so dark you cannot see, and why a flood of water covers you."

Some biblical justification exists for that idea. The stories of Uzzah and Nadab and Abihu tell us plainly that they died by the hand of God for their wickedness. The entire history of the nation of Israel is a history of God punishing them for doing evil and rewarding them for righteousness. In the New Testament we read the stories of Ananias and Sapphira and Elymas the sorcerer as examples of God's divine wrath evidenced against wickedness.

But even in Job there is the idea that suffering is part of the divine plan and that it has a divine purpose. Job says: "[W]hen he has tested me, I will come forth as gold" (Job 23:10). There is also the obvious truth that God does not always choose to inflict immediate, divine, physical retribution on every sinner. If He did, there wouldn't be anyone left alive. Ananias and Sapphira weren't the only liars in the Jerusalem congregation. If God had killed all of the liars in that church, there wouldn't have been a Jerusalem congregation.

It appears that God chooses to punish some sins and some people immediately and severely. He also chooses not to do that with others. On what basis He makes those choices He has not revealed to us.

James says in James 1:2-4: "Consider it pure joy, my brothers, whenever you face trials of many kinds, because you know that the testing of your faith develops perseverance. Perseverance must finish its work so that you may be mature and complete, not lacking anything." James says that trials are a testing of our faith. Who would be interested in testing our faith? Consider that if the intent of the testing is to develop perseverance, God would be interested in that. If the intent is to weaken or destroy our faith, then Satan would be interested. We have all experienced both of those results in the testing that has taken place in our lives and witnessed it in the lives of others. Satan's intent in wanting Job to be tested by suffering was to cause Job to curse God to His face. God's intent was to refine and increase Job's faith.

In James 1:12 James says: "Blessed is the man who perseveres under trial, because when he has stood the test, he will receive the crown of life that God has promised to those who love him." Here is where we run into great difficulty. We want to believe that suffering is caused by Satan because we simply cannot stand to believe that God would cause suffering. And sometimes it is caused by Satan—as in the case of Job and in the case of Paul's "thorn" which he refers to as a "messenger of Satan" (2 Corinthians 12:7).

But even in those cases Satan only does what God allows him to do, which means that God could have prevented their suffering and chose not to. Honesty demands that we ask ourselves: If suffering produces perseverance and perseverance makes the Christian mature and complete, why would Satan cause suffering if it defeats his purposes?

There are at least two possible answers to that question. First, this may be one of those areas where our finite minds are simply not capable of grasping how an infinite mind works. Second, under that overall understanding, it is possible that God chooses not to know the outcome of our suffering and that Satan cannot know? This seems to be the case in Job's suffering. That would mean that both God and Satan seek to use suffering to accomplish their purposes, and they wait anxiously to see the outcome.

We can be absolutely certain of these things: We have no choice about whether we suffer. Suffering is neither good nor bad in itself; it is the human condition. We do not know the outcome of our suffering. Neither God nor Satan chooses the outcome of our suffering—we do that.

Paul writes in Philippians 1:12: "[W]hat has happened to me has really served to advance the gospel." Paul did not choose the imprisonment, and he did not know the outcome when it happened. What he chose was his attitude toward it, and God was able to use it for His purposes. One of the most noble of all human sentiments toward suffering is found in Fyodor Dostoevsky's book *The Brothers Karamazov*. One of the author's heroes says, "God, help me to be worthy of my sufferings"—may that be said by all of us.

It is important to remember that suffering entered the world by the *specific will of God* when He delivered those initial curses upon Adam and Eve. Eve would have pain in childbirth, and her desire would be for her husband. Adam was condemned to earn his bread by the sweat of his brow. The promise of God that they would "surely die" is inherently painful (Genesis 2:17).

It would seem that if we have an abiding faith in the providence of God, we would see every event of our lives as the activity of God to bring us closer to Him. Israel's victory at Jericho and defeat at Ai are typical of the thousands of other biblical incidents recorded to indicate the purposeful activity of God in the lives of His people.

Suffering is not only part of what it means to be human; it is an integral part of the Christian life. Second Timothy 3:12 says: "In fact, everyone who wants to live a godly life in Christ Jesus will be persecuted." The specific biblical evidence of that truth is witnessed in the stoning of Stephen and the imprisonment and beating of Paul. Jesus tells His disciples in Matthew 10:22: "All men will hate you because of me." Perhaps when people come to us for baptism one of the questions we ought to ask them is if they are ready to suffer? The Christian historian Tertullian wrote, "Christians outlive, outthink and out-die all others. The blood of the martyrs is the seed of the kingdom."

Peter says that suffering is the key to ridding ourselves of sin. When I read a statement like that the first question that comes to my mind is, "God, isn't there perhaps some less painful way of accomplishing that?" What is the relationship between suffering and sinlessness? I would offer you this. The more suffering we have in this life, the less focused and attached we are to this world; therefore the less sinful we are.

In 1 Peter 3:17 Peter says: "It is better, if it is God's will, to suffer for doing good than for doing evil." Peter clearly states that our suffering could be the result of God's will. Because we know that God loves us beyond our comprehension, why would He either bring about circumstances that lead to suffering or at least not prevent those circumstances?

The answer to that question is that suffering is the key to having the mind of the Christ. Having the mind of Christ is God's will for our lives. It is relatively easy to recite the Lord's Prayer and say, "[Y]our will be done" (Matthew 6:10), when we believe that His will is going to be pleasant. The question is, would we still be able to say "[Y]our will be done" if we knew that it was going to mean hardship, disease, financial ruin, imprisonment, pain, suffering, and/or death? Do we realize what saying "[Y]our will be done" meant for Jesus (Matthew 26:42)? It meant a mockery of a trial, a severe beating, crucifixion, and death. It also meant a glorious resurrection and triumph over Satan.

Our problem is that we simply cannot bring ourselves to believe that suffering would be God's will. There are at least two major reasons for that.

1. The first is that we think of our lives only in material and finite terms while God thinks of them in eternal and spiritual terms.

2. The second is that our concept of love is so distorted by our culture and media that it leaves no room for the possibility that saying "no," although causing temporary pain might be more loving than saying "yes" and bringing temporary joy.

A good example of this is Paul and his "thorn" (2 Corinthians 12:7). Whatever the thorn was, it caused him much suffering; so much so that he asked God three times to remove it (v. 8). Think for a moment about what we know. We know that God loved Paul. We know that He could have healed Paul. We know that God had healed hundreds of people of every kind of disease and malady imaginable through the hands of this apostle.

The problem with that "knowledge" is that the prevalent cultural concept of love would mean that God *had* to heal him. God said "No!" He refused to because it was not His will. And what was His will? That Paul should be perfected through suffering. That he should develop the mind of the Christ and place his trust in God's wisdom and grace.

What possible motive could a loving God have for either causing or allowing tragic suffering among those whom He loves so much that He allowed His only Son to be murdered on their account?

I believe that the key to answering that question comes from the mouth of Jesus in John 17:1-3: "After Jesus said this, he looked toward heaven and prayed: 'Father, the time has come. Glorify your Son, that your Son may glorify you. For you granted him authority over all people that he might give eternal life to all those you have given him. Now this is eternal life: that they may know you, the only true God, and Jesus Christ, whom you have sent.'"

Normally when we think of salvation, we have some rather nebulous thoughts about heaven where the street is pure gold with gates of pearl and the tree of life (Revelation 21:21; 22:2). Jesus says that the whole idea of eternal life, salvation, and heaven is bound up in one thing—knowing God. We must open our minds to the possibility that the only reason why God created an immense universe—and in that universe He created a tiny speck of a planet that we call earth, and on that tiny speck of a planet He created some incredibly insignificant things called human beings—the only reason for all of that was to grant those human beings the possibility of eternal life. That was the focal point of His entire creation.

If we open our minds even further and understand that the reason for everything God has done since His creation was to teach those human beings to know Him as the means to that end of offering them eternal life, we begin to make progress in our search for understanding the purpose of suffering.

If God's only purpose in creation was to grant us the right to know Him, that means it was God's intention that man should find his entire reason for being, his peace, joy, and fulfillment, in that one all-consuming purpose. The prophet Jeremiah writes in Jeremiah 9:23, 24: "This is what the LORD says: 'Let not the wise man boast of his wisdom or the strong man boast of his strength or the rich man boast of his riches, but let him who boasts boast about this: that he understands and knows me, that I am the LORD, who exercises kindness, justice and righteousness on earth, for in these I delight,' declares the LORD."

Mark 10:17-23 (and also Luke 18:18-27) contains the story that we commonly refer to as the story of the rich ruler:

> As Jesus started on his way, a man ran up to him and fell on his knees before him. "Good teacher," he asked, "what must I do to inherit eternal life?" "Why do you call me good?" Jesus answered. "No one is good—except God alone. You know the commandments: 'Do not murder, do not commit adultery, do not steal, do not give false testimony, do not defraud, honor your father and mother.'" "Teacher," he declared, "all these I have kept since I was a boy." Jesus looked at him and loved him. "One thing you lack," he said. "Go, sell everything you have and give to the poor, and you will have treasure in heaven. Then come, follow me." At this the man's face fell. He went away sad, because he had great wealth. Jesus looked

around and said to his disciples, "How hard it is for the rich to enter the kingdom of God!"

The story of the rich ruler is familiar to most of us. It is intriguing to us for several reasons. Here is a man who genuinely wants to inherit eternal life. It is disconcerting to read that he has kept all of God's commandments, yet he is still lacking something. How is it possible to keep all of God's commandments and still be lacking something that is essential to eternal life? What could he possibly be lacking?

When he asks that question, Jesus does not give him any of the answers that we would anticipate. For instance, He doesn't tell him that faith, grace, baptism, penitence, unconditional love, or that his "commandment keeping" will save him. He says that he lacks one thing, but He tells him three things he needs to do to achieve the one thing. First, he has to go and sell everything he has. Second, he has to distribute the proceeds from the sale to the poor. Third, he has to follow Jesus.

The question is: What is the relationship between doing those three things and the answer to his question about how to inherit eternal life? If we look at the definition of eternal life that Jesus gives as "knowing God," we can see that the three things He tells him to do are tied to that purpose. That means that the "one thing" that he lacks is "knowing God," and the three things he has to do will accomplish that.

The rich ruler is told to sacrifice the things that are most valuable to him. What does that have to do with eternal life? If we equate eternal life with "knowing God," the answer becomes more obvious. Didn't God give up what was most valuable to Him for our sakes—His only Son? This man will never come to know God—have eternal life—until he sacrifices what is most valuable to himself—his wealth.

He is also told to distribute the proceeds to the poor, to people who don't deserve it and who have done nothing to earn it. Hasn't God distributed His wealth to people who don't deserve it—us? This rich ruler will never come to know God and never have the mind of Christ until he is able to identify with God's sacrifice for him. That means that he will never *know God* until he gives his most precious possessions to those who don't deserve it.

He is told to follow Jesus. Why? Because Jesus said that He came to "show us the Father" (John 14: 8, 9). If he follows Jesus, he will come to know God; that is what it takes to "inherit eternal life." I wonder which of these instructions sent him away sadly? I wonder which of them would send me away sadly? Would you sell everything you have and give it to the poor if you thought it was God's will and necessary to knowing Him and having eternal life? Of course we know the right answer. Do we realize what "being poor" would mean to the rich ruler? He would have to work. He would have to do the menial tasks that he now hires others to do. He would have to serve others—even wash their feet—instead of having them serve him.

I'm sure that this rich ruler suffered terribly with this decision. Remember that he genuinely wanted eternal life. I'm sure that he continued to suffer for the rest of his life as a result. My point is that that suffering would be God's will for his life; because God loves him so much that He will allow him to suffer, if that is what it takes to bring him to eternal life.

His wealth kept him from having the mind of the Christ. Instead of receiving the good news with eager thanksgiving and instead of him saying, "You mean that's all I have to do? I can't wait to get rid of my stuff"—he went away sadly. We learn in Luke 14:33 that Jesus expects all of us to do the same thing. "[A]ny of you who does not give up everything he has cannot be my disciple."

In 1 Peter 4:19 the Holy Spirit records: "So then, those who suffer according to God's will should commit themselves to their faithful Creator and continue to do good." Not only does God expect us to trust Him when we are suffering according to His will, He expects us to suffer bravely— to not sit and whine about how hard our lives are but to continue to serve others. Isn't that exactly what Jesus did His whole life? Isn't that exactly what the cross is about? Can we see that the only way we can have the mind of Christ and identify with Him is to live as He lived? That means that we must suffer as He suffered.

In John 12:27-29 Jesus is in the last two weeks of His life. It is just a few days before His trial, beating, and crucifixion. The movie *The Passion of the Christ* gives us some idea of what the physical part of that was like. Jesus knows exactly what is about to happen, and He knows that what is going to happen to Him is the will of God. He says: "[A]nd what shall I say? 'Father, save me from this hour'? No, it was for this very reason I came to this hour. Father, glorify your name!" (vv. 27-28).

What was the purpose that brought Jesus to the hour of His crucifixion? It was that God's will should be done and that His name should be glorified. That is God's purpose in all suffering—even yours and mine. I do not say that God's purpose is always done or that His name is always glorified, but that is His purpose.

CHAPTER 4

I want to return to James 1:2-4 because I have always struggled with it: "Consider it pure joy, my brothers, whenever you face trials of many kinds, because you know that the testing of your faith develops perseverance. Perseverance must finish its work so that you may be mature and complete, not lacking anything." James says that the purpose of suffering is to test our faith. If we think about it and look at biblical examples like Abraham and Isaac, we will realize that our faith cannot be tested in any other way.

But even with that understanding, how is it possible to consider it joy? Did Abraham offer Isaac cheerfully? I simply do not believe that! The "joy" is not in the testing or the suffering; it is in the consideration. It is in the anticipation of what God's testing is intended to accomplish. Testing accomplishes endurance, and endurance leads to perfection. Perfection is the knowledge of God; which Jesus said is what it means to have eternal life.

We may say that there ought not to be suffering, but there *is* suffering. It is inevitable, and it is not only integral to being human—it is the will of God. Suffering is not the worst thing that can happen to us. What is far worse than suffering?

1. It is to suffer without meaning or purpose.

2. It is to suffer and not grow from it; to suffer and not become more loving, kind, and compassionate, and more sanctified to God.

3. It is to suffer and not become more concerned about and sympathetic with other sufferers.

4. It is to suffer meaninglessly, and that is the worst thing that can happen to us.

5. If our suffering does not accomplish God's will and purposes—if it does not give us "the mind of Christ"—then it is for nothing.

Suffering will either bring out the best or the worst in us. Suffering either takes us out of ourselves and deeper into the will of God or it brings us more deeply into ourselves and out of the will of God. Suffering either creates sympathy for other sufferers and causes us to forget ourselves and serve them, or it creates a morbid focus on our own problems. Self-centered suffering turns us into complainers and whiners who believe that our pain, sickness, and suffering are greater than anyone else's and makes us insensitive to the pain of others. We are all aware of those who have no time to listen to or sympathize with the suffering and grief of others. We hate to tell them about our struggles because they can't wait for us to finish so they can say: "Oh, that's nothing; wait till I tell you what happened to me." Suffering either accomplishes God's purposes or Satan's purposes. It's our choice.

Peter says that because the Christ suffered in the flesh we should prepare our minds with the same attitude toward suffering that the Christ had. In Matthew 16:21-23 Peter takes Jesus aside and rebukes Him because He has been talking about suffering and dying. He essentially says, "Lord, you have got to stop talking about suffering and dying. Don't you understand that nobody is going to follow you if you keep talking that way? You've got to talk about power, winning, triumph. That's what people want to hear." Jesus says, "Get behind me, Satan! You are a stumbling block to me; you do not have in mind the things of God, but the things of men" (v. 23).

Questions for 1 Peter 4:1-6 (Part 1)

1. What attitude did the Christ have toward suffering?
2. The stories of Uzzah and Nadab and Abihu tell us plainly that they died by the hand of God for their wickedness. Do you think that God still inflicts suffering as punishment for sin?
3. James says that trials are a testing of our faith (James 1:2-4). Why might a Christian desire to have his faith tested?
4. Why would Satan cause suffering if it defeats his purposes?
5. How did suffering enter the world?
6. Peter says that suffering is the key to ridding ourselves of sin. What is the relationship between suffering and sinlessness?
7. What attitude did Job and his friends have toward suffering?
8. Is suffering ever the result of God's will?
9. Can God prevent suffering? If so, why doesn't He?
10. What possible motive could a loving God have for either causing or allowing tragic suffering among those whom He loves so much that He allowed His only Son to be murdered on their account?
11. How is it possible to keep all of God's commandments and still be lacking something that is essential to eternal life?
12. In the story of the rich ruler, Jesus tells him three things he has to do to inherit eternal life. What is the relationship between these three things and inheriting eternal life?
13. What does sacrificing the things that are most valuable to him have to do with the rich ruler's eternal life?

14. The rich ruler is also told to distribute the proceeds of selling all his riches to the poor—to people who don't deserve it—and to follow Jesus. Why?

15. What was the purpose that brought Jesus to the hour of His crucifixion?

16. How is it possible to consider trials joy? Did Abraham offer Isaac cheerfully?

17. Discuss these statements: "Suffering will either bring out the best or the worst in us. Suffering either takes us out of ourselves and deeper into the will of God or it brings us more deeply into ourselves and out of the will of God. Suffering either creates sympathy for other sufferers and causes us to forget ourselves and serve them, or it creates a morbid focus on our own problems."

Therefore, since Christ suffered in his body, arm yourselves also with the same attitude, because he who has suffered in his body is done with sin. As a result, he does not live the rest of his earthly life for evil human desires, but rather for the will of God. For you have spent enough time in the past doing what pagans choose to do—living in debauchery, lust, drunkenness, orgies, carousing and detestable idolatry. They think it strange that you do not plunge with them into the same flood of dissipation, and they heap abuse on you. But they will have to give account to him who is ready to judge the living and the dead. For this is the reason the gospel was preached even to those who are now dead, so that they might be judged according to men in regard to the body, but live according to God in regard to the spirit (1 Peter 4:1-6).

Part 2

The more we love other people not only are the *chances* of our suffering increased, but the *depth* of our suffering is also increased. The Christ suffered more than any man because He understood sin and condemnation better than any man and loved more than any man. When we put on the mind of the Christ we will suffer with Him and for the same reasons that He suffered.

Second Corinthians 1:3-7 contains two extremely challenging thoughts. Paul writes

Praise be to the God and Father of our Lord Jesus Christ, the Father

of compassion and the God of all comfort, who comforts us in all
our troubles, so that we can comfort those in any trouble with
the comfort we ourselves have received from God. For just as the
sufferings of Christ flow over into our lives, so also through Christ
our comfort overflows. If we are distressed, it is for your comfort and
salvation; if we are comforted, it is for your comfort, which produces
in you patient endurance of the same sufferings we suffer. And our
hope for you is firm, because we know that just as you share in our
sufferings, so also you share in our comfort.

Paul says that one of the purposes of our suffering is that when
we experience the comfort that God grants to His suffering children;
we as His children can be instrumental in comforting others. He also
says that just as the sufferings of Christ flow over into our lives so also
His comfort overflows. What does it mean for Christ's sufferings to
flow over into our lives? I believe it means that the more we identify
with His love for mankind, the more we will suffer as He did and for
the same reasons. We are more sensitive to sin and to the meaning of
being lost.

Listen to the suffering Christ as He grieves over the city of Jerusalem
in Matthew 23:37-40: "O Jerusalem, Jerusalem, you who kill the prophets
and stone those sent to you, how often I have longed to gather your
children together, as a hen gathers her chicks under her wings, but
you were not willing. Look, your house is left to you desolate. For I tell
you, you will not see me again until you say, 'Blessed is he who comes
in the name of the Lord.' " When we suffer for the same reasons He
suffered, we will also be comforted by what comforted Him—doing
God's will.

Peter writes in 1 Peter 4:12, 13: "Dear friends, do not be surprised at
the painful trial you are suffering, as though something strange were
happening to you. But rejoice that you participate in the sufferings of
Christ, so that you may be overjoyed when his glory is revealed." The
Holy Spirit says that there is a vital relationship between our suffering
and our identification with Jesus. The sufferings of Christ flow over into
our lives through our identification with those sufferings. We identify
with His sufferings when we suffer with Him and for Him, when we feel
His pain, display His love and share in His disappointment. That is the
purpose of all suffering—to bring us into identification with Jesus.

Paul writes in Romans 8:17: "Now if we are children, then we are
heirs—heirs of God and co-heirs with Christ, if indeed we share in his

sufferings in order that we may also share in his glory." Our identity with Jesus is tested and proved by our willingness to "share" in the family sorrows. Sharing in the family sorrows allows us the privilege of sharing in the family joys.

In Philippians 3:10 Paul writes: "I want to know Christ and the power of his resurrection and the fellowship of sharing in his sufferings, becoming like him in his death." When Paul speaks of his fervent desire to know the Christ, he understands that he can only come to eternal life, holiness, and sanctification through the knowledge of God. He does not mean knowledge about God (although that is vitally important), but he wants his knowledge about God to be incorporated into his experience of God that comes through his identification with Jesus Christ. The knowing that is possible for us in this life can only come to us when we identify with Jesus, and that is why Paul wants to share in His sufferings—so that he can experience the "power of his resurrection."

There is an irony in all human existence that creates a direct relationship between opposites. Love stands opposed to hate. Peace stands opposed to strife. Health stands opposed to sickness. Gratitude stands opposed to ingratitude. Heat stands opposed to cold. Our ability to appreciate love, peace, health, happiness, or gratitude is in direct proportion to the extent we have experienced their counterparts. To the extent that we identify with the death and suffering of Jesus we are able to identify with His resurrection life and "the joy set before him" (Hebrews 12:2).

In Colossians 1:24 Paul, through the Holy Spirit, records: "Now I rejoice in what was suffered for you, and I fill up in my flesh what is still lacking in regard to Christ's afflictions, for the sake of his body, which is the church." What could possibly still be lacking in the afflictions of Christ? The Hebrew writer says: "Although he was a son, he learned obedience from what he suffered" (Hebrews 5:8).

If Jesus had to learn obedience through suffering, is it possible that we could learn it without suffering? We cannot learn obedience through the sufferings of the Christ. We must learn obedience through our own suffering. That is what is lacking in the sufferings of Jesus. If Jesus had to learn trust through suffering, is it possible that we could learn it without suffering? If Jesus had to learn to love through suffering, is it possible that we could learn it without suffering? If Jesus had to learn contentment in disappointment through suffering, is it possible that we could learn it without suffering?

Paul is saying that the incredible accumulation of the sufferings of Jesus for us and for the will of God does not mean that there is no more to be accomplished through that medium. The fact that Jesus suffered for us means that we must suffer for Him and for the church and the gospel for which He died.

Suffering is God's refining fire, and we will never truly identify with Jesus and the cross until we suffer. The deeper our suffering the greater our identification with the cross. Suffering burns what is trivial and shallow from our lives and puts us in touch with what it means to love God with all our hearts.

Questions for 1 Peter 4:1-6 (Part 2)

1. Discuss this statement: The more we love other people, not only are the *chances* of our suffering increased but the *depth* of our suffering is also increased.
2. In Colossians 1:24 Paul refers to "what is still lacking in regard to Christ's afflictions." What could possibly still be lacking in the afflictions of Christ?

The end of all things is near. Therefore be clear minded and self-controlled so that you can pray. Above all, love each other deeply, because love covers over a multitude of sins. Offer hospitality to one another without grumbling. Each one should use whatever gift he has received to serve others, faithfully administering God's grace in its various forms. If anyone speaks, he should do it as one speaking the very words of God. If anyone serves, he should do it with the strength God provides, so that in all things God may be praised through Jesus Christ. To him be the glory and the power for ever and ever. Amen (1 Peter 4:7-11).

"The end of all things is near." The end is always at hand either because of our physical death or the second coming of the Lord. Peter's instruction to Christians to be "clear minded and self-controlled" means that Christians should be more in touch with the realities of life and the illusory nature of the material world. We should also be aware of and on the lookout for the cunning schemes of Satan to destroy us—"so that you can pray" (1 Peter 4:7). Our prayer life should be focused on spiritual realities—not physical ones.

The deep love that Peter talks about means that our love for each other must cover our differences and our faults. Fervent love covers sins. To cover means to hide from view. Here it means that our love refuses to display the faults of others. It also means that our love takes no account, or does not allow those faults to interfere with fellowship or forgiveness.

We are to be hospitable. Probably one of the greatest areas of weakness in our fellowship is hospitality. It means to have a welcoming and gracious attitude that is manifested by having people in your home. It is a requirement for elders, but it rarely is considered when we select them. I've never heard of a man being rejected from serving as an elder for failing to be hospitable.

We must use our gifts to build up the community of saints not to further our own interests. When Peter says, "If anyone speaks" (1 Peter 4:11), he means if anyone teaches, instructs, or edifies the congregation, let that teaching and edification be based upon God's revealed will. If anyone ministers or serves others, let it be done in such a way that God gets the glory for it. It is good to look at verse 17 here. The statement "For it is time" is tied directly to verse 7. If you skip the verses in between, you can see the continuity. "[F]or judgment to begin with the family of God" (v. 17).

Questions for 1 Peter 4:7-11

1. Why should we be "clear minded and self-controlled"?
2. What does Peter mean when he tells us to "love each other deeply" and "offer hospitality to one another"? What are specific ways we can accomplish these things?

Dear friends, do not be surprised at the painful trial you are suffering, as though something strange were happening to you. But rejoice that you participate in the sufferings of Christ, so that you may be overjoyed when his glory is revealed. If you are insulted because of the name of Christ, you are blessed, for the Spirit of glory and of God rests on you. If you suffer, it should not be as a murderer or thief or any other kind of criminal, or even as a meddler. However, if you suffer as a Christian, do not be ashamed, but praise God that you bear that name. For it is

time for judgment to begin with the family of God; and if it begins with us, what will the outcome be for those who do not obey the gospel of God? And, "If it is hard for the righteous to be saved, what will become of the ungodly and the sinner?" So then, those who suffer according to God's will should commit themselves to their faithful Creator and continue to do good (1 Peter 4:12-19).

Please review my comments earlier in this chapter on 1 Peter 4:1-6 (Part 2) on what it means to "participate in the sufferings of Christ." I would add here that it means to take part in, to share in, and to so identify with the Christ that we experience what He experienced. How do we do that? Obviously, we are not going to be crucified, scourged, or tried as He was. But the greatest sufferings of Jesus were not in the physical things He endured. They were in the spiritual things.

1. Think about how He felt in John 6 when He asked the Twelve, "You do not want to leave too, do you?"

2. Think about how He felt in Gethsemane when He asked Peter, James, and John: "Could you men not keep watch with me for one hour?" (Matthew 26:40).

3. Think about what He was feeling when He looked over the city of God and said, "O Jerusalem, Jerusalem" (Matthew 23:37; Luke 13:34).

4. Think about what He was feeling when He turned and spoke to those weeping women who were following Him through the streets of Jerusalem and said, "[D]o not weep for me; weep for yourselves and for your children" (Luke 23:28).

5. Think about what He was feeling when He said, "Father, forgive them, for they do not know what they are doing" (Luke 23:34).

6. Think about the disappointment He was feeling when He said to the frustrated sister of Mary, "Martha, Martha ... you are worried and upset about many things" (Luke 10:41).

7. Think about the disappointment and suffering He felt when He said to His disciples, "Are you still so dull?" (Matthew 15:16) and "Have you no room for my words find no place in you?" (John 8:37).

We can participate in the sufferings of the Christ when we experience those feelings. We can feel what He felt when He saw sin, evil, destruction, greed, and lust. We can *grieve* as He did at the tomb of Lazarus.

Peter says that when Jesus comes back, those who have been purified and sanctified through suffering will participate in His glory. Anything we may have suffered will seem as nothing in comparison with the reward God has in store for us. When Peter says that "it is time for judgment to begin with the family of God" (1 Peter 4:17), he means severe trial. The "family of God" denotes the church. A time of severe trial and persecution was going to come upon the church. The idea presented by: "If it is hard for the righteous to be saved, what will become of the ungodly and the sinner?" (v. 18) can be taken two ways. First, "saved" may not refer to the final judgment but to the imminent persecution. Second, Peter may be saying that the salvation of the righteous was hard because it cost Jesus the crucifixion. If it took the death of the Messiah to save the righteous, the unrighteous don't have a chance.

Questions for 1 Peter 4:12-19

1. The greatest sufferings of Christ were not the physical things He endured but in the spiritual things. Can you recall some of His spiritual sufferings noted in this chapter?
2. Who is the "family of God"?

FIRST PETER

FIRST PETER
CHAPTER 5

To the elders among you, I appeal as a fellow elder, a witness of Christ's sufferings and one who also will share in the glory to be revealed: Be shepherds of God's flock that is under your care, serving as overseers— not because you must, but because you are willing, as God wants you to be; not greedy for money, but eager to serve; not lording it over those entrusted to you, but being examples to the flock. And when the Chief Shepherd appears, you will receive the crown of glory that will never fade away (1 Peter 5:1-4).

Peter says that he witnessed Christ's sufferings. We must not overlook the influence that must have had on his attitude.

Peter turns his attention to the elders in the congregations he addresses. One of the most interesting things about elders is not what Peter says but what he does not say. Because Peter writes what we call a "general epistle," that is, one not sent to any specific person or congregation, it leads us to wonder to what elders he is referring?

It is interesting to note that Paul's epistles to the congregations in Galatia, Ephesus, Colossae, Thessalonica, Rome, and Corinth make no mention of elders or deacons. It is also interesting to note that the qualifications that Paul gives for elders and deacons are not sent to congregations but to evangelists. It certainly appears that Peter is saying that *he* is an elder in the same designated sense that we think of them today. But that leads us to ask, if Peter was a traveling evangelist, for what congregation was he an elder? If he wasn't an elder in a specific congregation, is it possible that he was an elder "at large"?

In Acts 20:17, 18, 28-30 Luke records

From Miletus, Paul sent to Ephesus for the elders of the church. When they arrived, he said to them: ... "Keep watch over yourselves and all the flock of which the Holy Spirit has made you overseers. Be shepherds of the church of God, which he bought with his own blood. I know that after I leave, savage wolves will come in among you and will not spare the flock. Even from your own number men will arise and distort the truth in order to draw away disciples after them."

The following are some important questions for discussion: Ephesus was a very large city—well over two hundred thousand at the time of Paul's writing. It is hard to believe that every member of the church in Ephesus worshiped at the same location, yet Paul speaks of the "church" in Ephesus in a collective sense. Is it possible that the city of Ephesus had only one set of elders who served several house churches?

Paul exhorts the elders first of all to "[k]eep watch over" themselves. Only after they have looked to themselves are they to watch over all the flock. We need to ask ourselves: What is involved in the self-examination implied in the "[k]eep watch over yourselves" instruction? What do they need to be on guard against? What kinds of temptations are elders particularly subject to?

Peter tells elders to shepherd "the church of God." What does that mean? Does shepherding imply that elders should do for the members of the congregation what a shepherd does for his flock? If the main responsibilities of a shepherd are to keep the flock well fed; to protect them from harm and outside influences; to heal their wounds; to comfort and discipline them; and to help them to lead productive lives; how do they do that?

1. They must lead them by their example of what *they* eat.

2. They must stay away from danger themselves.

3. They must warn them by teaching them.

4. They must be good physicians in applying the medicine that the sheep need to bring about healing. That medicine may be prayer, spiritual counsel, financial assistance, Bible study, or a hug.

Paul goes on to say that "the Holy Spirit has made you overseers" (Acts 20:28). How did the Holy Spirit do that? Let me offer the following ways He might have done that:

1. by helping them to understand the Bible (1 Corinthians 2)

2. by leading them (Romans 8)

3. by gifting and preparing them for this position

4. by calling them to it

5. by giving inspired guidelines to evangelists for appointing them

6. by promoting the "fruit of the Spirit" in their lives (Galatians 5)

Paul ends his exhortation to elders by saying that the greatest threat to the welfare of the congregations they serve will come from within the eldership itself.

In 1 Peter 5:2 Peter tells elders that they are not board members, chief executive officers, or office managers. They are visionary, spiritual, inspirational leaders who demonstrate what needs to be done. Peter's instruction to "[b]e shepherds of God's flock that is under your care," indicates that there may be flocks that are not under their care.

"[S]erving as overseers" (1 Peter 5:2). The "overseer" is one who has a vision of what is good for the entire congregation—not just the older, or younger, or middle aged, or any other special interest group, like those who are liberal or conservative. It means that the elder is to have a perspective on both corporate and individual needs. Not only should he keep the welfare of every member in mind, he must also make sure that his flock has a kingdom view and kingdom loyalty—not just a local, congregational one.

Elders are to be "overseers," not because they have been talked into it or made to feel guilty for not doing it, but because they feel called to it and are willing to accept the challenge. Elders are not to be "greedy for money, but eager to serve" (1 Peter 5:2). Peter is very concerned about the motives that men have for becoming and for remaining an elder. Every elder needs to periodically reexamine his motives.

Elders are not to lord it over those who are entrusted to them. They are to be examples to the flock. Why the warning? Because the position lends itself to authoritarianism, dictatorial attitudes, and autocratic decision-making. The more institutional the congregation becomes the more potential there is for "lording it over."

There is no inherent authority in the position of elder. All spiritual authority in the church is vested in the Scriptures. Elders have authority only as they wield the sword of the Spirit. The only material and practical authority they have is what the congregation grants them. For instance, as far as the Bible is concerned, elders have no authority over financial matters unless the congregation specifically asks them to handle the financial affairs. And even then the congregation can withdraw that authority any time they wish and assign it to whomever they wish.

Elders face the very difficult task of leading the congregation without having either inherent or personal authority. No congregation will ever rise above its leadership. James 5:14, 15 gives a good picture of the practical work of elders: "Is any one of you sick? He should call the elders of the church to pray over him and anoint him with oil in the name of the Lord. And the prayer offered in faith will make the sick person well; the Lord will raise him up. If he has sinned, he will be forgiven."

Questions for 1 Peter 5:1-4

1. Paul exhorts the elders to "[k]eep watch over" themselves (Acts 20:28). Only after they have looked to themselves are they to keep watch over "all the flock." We need to ask ourselves:

   • What is involved in the self examination implied in the "[k]eep watch over yourselves" instruction?

   • What do they need to "[k]eep watch" against?

   • What kinds of temptations particularly affect elders?

2. Why do you suppose there is nothing in Scripture that lends itself to the idea that elders are decision makers?

3. Paul tells elders to "[b]e shepherds of the church of God" (Acts 20:28). What does that mean?

4. Does shepherding imply that elders should do for the members of the congregation what a shepherd does for his flock of sheep?

5. If the main responsibilities of a shepherd are to keep the flock well fed; to protect them from harm and outside influences; to heal their wounds; to comfort and discipline them; and to help them to lead productive lives—how should elders do that?

6. What is the work of an "overseer"?

7. Do you believe that there is inherent authority ("because I said so") in the position of elder? Why?

8. What does it mean to lord it over (1 Peter 5:3)? Why does Peter warn elders against it?

Young men, in the same way be submissive to those who are older. All of you, clothe yourselves with humility toward one another, because, "God opposes the proud but gives grace to the humble." Humble yourselves, therefore, under God's mighty hand, that he may lift you

CHAPTER 5

up in due time. Cast all your anxiety on him because he cares for you (1 Peter 5:5-7).

Peter exhorts the young men of the congregation to submit to those "who are older." It is interesting how few things have changed over the centuries. Peter would not have given the exhortation if there had been no problem. I suppose that every congregation of God's people has faced the problem of young people wanting to make changes, and old people wanting things to stay the same. Obviously no congregation can have it both ways; and the job of the elders is to teach and exhibit the "humility" that is essential to keep young and old alike focused on reaching the lost, rather than pleasing themselves. Any congregation that does not serve its young families is a dying congregation.

When Peter says "[a]ll of you," he means that an attitude of submission and humility must characterize the entire congregation: elders, evangelists, deacons, worship leaders, class teachers, young, old, men, women, and children alike. Our willingness to submit to each other is a result of our willingness to submit to God. We "humble" ourselves when we acknowledge God's superior wisdom, His superior justice, His salvation, His peace, His righteousness, and His grace. If we really understood how "amazing" grace is, we would find it more amazing than we ever imagined. Peter reminds us that God cares about us. What a constant comfort. When Moses held his staff out over the Red Sea, he said to the fainting Israelites: "Do not be afraid. Stand firm and you will see the deliverance the LORD will bring you today" (Exodus 14:13).

Be self-controlled and alert. Your enemy the devil prowls around like a roaring lion looking for someone to devour. Resist him, standing firm in the faith, because you know that your brothers throughout the world are undergoing the same kind of sufferings (1 Peter 5:8, 9).

Peter says that the devil is real, and he is looking for an opportunity. Satan cannot *create* opportunities; he can only *seize* them. James says in 1:13-15: "When tempted, no one should say, 'God is tempting me.' For God cannot be tempted by evil, nor does he tempt anyone; but each one is tempted when, by his own evil desire, he is dragged away and enticed. Then, after desire has conceived, it gives birth to sin; and sin, when it is full-grown, gives birth to death."

Peter says, "Resist him" (1 Peter 5:9). That means that we can. James

4:7 reads: "Submit yourselves, then, to God. Resist the devil, and he will flee from you." We resist first by knowing our areas of weakness. Satan will only attack us where we are weak. Satan has no real power. He cannot force us to do anything. Satan only has the power of illusion. He creates an illusion to tempt us in our area of weakness.

What practical methods do we use to resist? We need to confront sin in our lives by calling it by its name. It's not a mistake. It's not an error in judgment. We need to admit that what we have done is a sin, rather than trying to find ways of rationalizing or justifying it. We always need to flee from it, as Joseph did (Genesis 39:12).

"Know that your brothers throughout the world are undergoing the same kind of sufferings" (1 Peter 5:9). We need to remember that other people are suffering both from temptation and sin. Other people are tempted. Note 1 Corinthians 10:13: "No temptation has seized you except what is common to man. And God is faithful; he will not let you be tempted beyond what you can bear. But when you are tempted, he will also provide a way out so that you can stand up under it." Other people have problems. They are lonely, depressed, and discouraged. The more we concentrate on helping others, the less time we have to dwell on our problems.

And the God of all grace, who called you to his eternal glory in Christ, after you have suffered a little while, will himself restore you and make you strong, firm and steadfast. To him be the power for ever and ever. Amen. With the help of Silas, whom I regard as a faithful brother, I have written to you briefly, encouraging you and testifying that this is the true grace of God. Stand fast in it. She who is in Babylon, chosen together with you, sends you her greetings, and so does my son Mark. Greet one another with a kiss of love. Peace to all of you who are in Christ (1 Peter 5:10-14).

"[T]he God of all grace." Everything that we receive from God is an act of grace because we do not deserve it. Part of what we receive is suffering. "[A]fter you have suffered" God will restore you, making you "strong, firm and steadfast" (1 Peter 5:10). Notice that God does these things *after* we have suffered—not before. In fact, it is through those very sufferings that God provides restoration because it is impossible to be restored until we have been displaced by suffering.

"[T]his is the true grace of God" (1 Peter 5:12). Peter distinguishes between God's grace and grace that is attributed to God but is not His. How do we identify the "true grace" of God? Any grace that doesn't include suffering and restoration is not the true grace of God. Any grace which speaks only of health and wealth is not the true grace of God. Any grace which speaks only of winning—of success, blue skies and rainbows—is not the true grace of God.

We really don't know whom Peter refers to as being in Babylon. Some have conjectured that "[s]he" was Peter's wife, and Babylon means Rome. The reference may also be to some other saintly woman and/or some other town. We may be sure that those who received the letter knew who Peter was talking about and the place to which he was referring.

Questions for 1 Peter 5:5-14

1. How should we deal with the problem of young people wanting to make changes and old people wanting things to stay the same?

2. How can we resist the devil?

3. What is one of Satan's greatest powers?

4. What encouragement is there in knowing that other people are suffering both from temptation and sin?

5. How do we identify the "true grace" of God?

FIRST PETER

INTRODUCTION TO
SECOND PETER

Peter specifically identifies both himself and his audience in 2 Peter 1:1. He greets them much in the same manner as Paul does in his letters. The identification of the audience indicates that this is a "general epistle"—a letter to all Christians in the area to which it was sent rather than to a specific person or congregation.

Second Peter is an exhortation to diligence in reaching for a higher level of godliness. It is a reminder of what God has called us to. We learn in 2 Peter 1:13, 14 that Peter is writing in anticipation of his death. "I think it is right to refresh your memory as long as I live in the tent of this body, because I know that I will soon put it aside, as our Lord Jesus Christ has made clear to me." He intended that his words would serve all succeeding generations by goading them and bringing them back to the fundamentals of Christianity. "And I will make every effort to see that after my departure you will always be able to remember these things" (v. 15).

We all want to leave things of importance behind. We want our children to know who we were, the things we suffered and learned, and what we believed. Christians need to record their history—especially their faith history. It is often counterproductive to leave our children material possessions. Solomon says that often people labor all of their lives to leave things to their children without knowing if they will be wise or foolish (Ecclesiastes 2:18, 19). It's a poignant example because Solomon's son was a fool who lost most of what his father left him in a very short period of time.

We all need to be reminded periodically—especially spiritually—and that is the purpose of this book. In 2 Peter 1:12, Peter says: "So I will always remind you of these things, even though you know them and are firmly established in the truth you now have." Later, Peter writes:

"But do not forget this one thing, dear friends: With the Lord a day is like a thousand years, and a thousand years are like a day. The Lord is not slow in keeping his promise, as some understand slowness. He is patient with you, not wanting anyone to perish, but everyone to come to repentance" (3:8, 9).

First Peter deals with suffering produced by external circumstances and persecution. Second Peter deals with problems that come from inside the community of faith and inside the individual.

SECOND PETER
CHAPTER 1

Simon Peter, a servant and apostle of Jesus Christ, To those who through the righteousness of our God and Savior Jesus Christ have received a faith as precious as ours: Grace and peace be yours in abundance through the knowledge of God and of Jesus our Lord (2 Peter 1:1, 2).

It seems significant to me that Peter identifies himself first as a servant and second as an apostle. Peter is more concerned about his relationship with God as a servant than about his relationship with other Christians as an apostle.

Peter addresses himself to all of those who have *received* a "precious" faith. There are two things here worth noting, the first is that faith is "precious." Only faith can sustain us in our darkest hours—in financial distress; when our marriages are falling apart; when our health or that of loved ones is threatened; and when death approaches. The second is that we do not normally think of faith as something we "receive"; we are prone to think of faith as something we initiate and sustain by an act of our will. In 1 Corinthians 4:7 Paul writes: "For who makes you different from anyone else? What do you have that you did not receive? And if you did receive it, why do you boast as though you did not?"

In what way is faith "received"? God initiates our relationship with Him. John says in 1 John 4:10: "This is love: not that we loved God, but that he loved us." Faith is our response to God's approach. It is God who first seeks us, not us seeking Him. It is God who made faith possible by creating mankind with the capacity for belief. Peter writes to those who have accepted God's gift. It is Jesus who has given us something to believe in by dying on the cross.

Obedient faith is the result of the convicting work of the Holy Spirit.

Note John 16:5-11

"Now I am going to him who sent me, yet none of you asks me, 'Where are you going?' Because I have said these things, you are filled with grief. But I tell you the truth: It is for your good that I am going away. Unless I go away, the Counselor will not come to you; but if I go, I will send him to you. When he comes, he will convict the world of guilt in regard to sin and righteousness and judgment: in regard to sin, because men do not believe in me; in regard to righteousness, because I am going to the Father, where you can see me no longer; and in regard to judgment, because the prince of this world now stands condemned."

Our faith is the result of the faithfulness and righteousness of God. God has kept His promise to Abraham that in his seed all nations would be blessed by sending Jesus to us. Grace and peace are ours in direct proportion to our "knowledge" of God and His Son (2 Peter 1:2).

His divine power has given us everything we need for life and godliness through our knowledge of him who called us by his own glory and goodness. Through these he has given us his very great and precious promises, so that through them you may participate in the divine nature and escape the corruption in the world caused by evil desires (2 Peter 1:3, 4).

It is important to notice that God's divine power has given to Christians all that we *need*—not all that we *want*. What God gives us is further qualified by the purpose for which He gives it: "for life and godliness." God's blessings are not for material success or for health and happiness. His blessings supply what is necessary to achieve godliness.

Peter suggests that we can participate in the "divine nature" (2 Peter 1:4). It is very hard to get our minds wrapped around that concept—so hard in fact, that most of us probably don't take it very seriously. Being like God is an awe-inspiring idea and something greatly to be desired; but like all great ideas, making them a reality demands a price that few wish to pay. Sometimes we want to not only be *like* God, we want to *be* God. We want that because deep inside us—but certainly never voiced—exists the notion that we are not quite satisfied with the way things are going, and we think that although running the universe might be a little too much for us, we could do a better job with the day-to-day events of our lives than He does. One of the reasons for that feeling is that we do not see all ends because we look at events and circumstances from a self-centered and earthly point of view.

What does it mean to "participate in the divine nature" (2 Peter 1:4)? It means to be like God. And what is God like? He is holy. Holiness is purity. It means to be focused on one thing; it means to be set apart for a single purpose. It is only through holiness that we can "escape the corruption in the world." Holiness cannot be obtained unless we first are willing to deny ourselves. We cannot be focused on what we want and focused on what God wants at the same time.

God is not primarily concerned with our health, length of life, or our happiness. He has only one concern: our salvation. Peter says that participating in the divine nature can only be achieved through God's "great and precious promises" (2 Peter 1:4). What are those promises?

1. He has promised the indwelling Holy Spirit. In Acts 2:38, 39 Peter said: "Repent and be baptized, every one of you, in the name of Jesus Christ for the forgiveness of your sins. And you will receive the gift of the Holy Spirit. The promise is for you and your children and for all who are far off—for all whom the Lord our God will call."

2. Second Corinthians 6:16 states God's promise: "I will live with them and walk among them, and I will be their God, and they will be my people." Verse 18 adds, "I will be a Father to you, and you will be my sons and daughters, says the Lord Almighty."

3. Hebrews 8:10 tells us that God promises to "put my laws in their minds and write them on their hearts. I will be their God, and they will be my people."

4. Second Timothy 1:1: "Paul, an apostle of Christ Jesus by the will of God, according to the promise of life that is in Christ Jesus."

5. Hebrews 4:1: "Therefore, since the promise of entering his rest still stands, ..."

6. Second Peter 3:13: "But in keeping with his promise we are looking forward to a new heaven and a new earth, the home of righteousness."

Peter says that these "divine promises" will allow us to escape the corruption that is in the world if we incorporate them into our lives by faith. Of course, escaping the corruption that is in the world means that we will also lose some of the pleasures the world affords. I fear that too often we are willing to accept a little corruption to have the pleasures. Every person who spends money in Las Vegas supports the corruption, lewdness, vulgarity, immorality, and crime that form the foundation of the entire economy of that city. Every person who supports the lottery participates in the manipulation and deception it is based on. The question is not, "Can we have those great and precious promises?" The question is, "Do we really want them, and are we willing to pay the price it takes to have them?"

I want to focus briefly on one of the most far-reaching of those promises I mentioned above: the indwelling Holy Spirit. Paul writes in Galatians 5:16-25,

> So I say, live by the Spirit, and you will not gratify the desires of the sinful nature. For the sinful nature desires what is contrary to the Spirit, and the Spirit what is contrary to the sinful nature. They are in conflict with each other, so that you do not do what you want. But if you are led by the Spirit, you are not under law. The acts of the sinful nature are obvious: sexual immorality, impurity and debauchery; idolatry and witchcraft; hatred, discord, jealousy, fits of rage, selfish ambition, dissensions, factions and envy; drunkenness, orgies, and the like. I warn you, as I did before, that those who live like this will not inherit the kingdom of God. But the fruit of the Spirit is love, joy, peace, patience, kindness, goodness, faithfulness, gentleness and self-control. Against such things there is no law. Those who belong to Christ Jesus have crucified the sinful nature with its passions and desires. Since we live by the Spirit, let us keep in step with the Spirit.

Here is a promise that defies the imagination. But there are implications in that promise that make us wary. Does being controlled by the Holy Spirit mean that I have to give up my need to be in control? Does it mean that I give up my freedom to do what I want to do?

The voice of the flesh—the sinful nature—in all of us says: "Be careful. All of this sounds good, but remember that if you claim these promises, you are going to have to give up some things you love: your pride, your selfishness, and some really nice material things that you enjoy."

There is much in the Bible about self-denial. Many of the parables deal with it. Jesus said: "If anyone would come after me, he must deny himself and take up his cross and follow me" (Matthew 16:24). He also said: "For I have come down from heaven not to do my will but to do the will of him who sent me" (John 6:38). When Jesus washed the disciples' feet, Peter said: "[Y]ou shall never wash my feet" (John 13:8). Why was Peter so against that? Could it be that if He allowed Jesus to wash his feet, he might feel obligated to do the same for others? Jesus said, "Unless I wash [your feet], you have no part with me." What does that mean? It means that Christianity is a lifetime of washing feet.

We have problems with self-denial because we are bombarded with materialistic rationales about self-fulfillment, self-realization, and self-actualization. Common sayings like "Do your own thing," "It works for me," and "If it feels good, do it" are indications of a culture dominated by self-interests. What is good for me and for my happiness becomes the criterion for all decision making. The stories about the rich ruler, the good Samaritan, and the rich man and Lazarus all have something to say to us about self-denial.

Holiness means to see life as He saw it, to see people as He saw them, to see this world as He saw it; and holiness is to love as He loved. Holiness is not only sinlessness; it is the absence of the desire to sin.

Questions for 2 Peter 1:1-4

1. Why does Peter identify himself as a servant first and an apostle second?

2. How do we identify ourselves?

3. Why does Peter speak of faith as something we "receive"?

4. In what way is faith received?

5. What does it mean to participate in the divine nature?

6. Peter says that participating in the divine nature can only be achieved through God's "great and precious promises." Think of all God's promises and make a list.

7. Why do we think that although running the universe might be a little too much for us, we could do a better job than God with the day-to-day events of our lives?

8. What does it mean to be controlled by the Holy Spirit?

9. How do God's "divine promises" allow us to escape the corruption that is in the world?

For this very reason, make every effort to add to your faith goodness; and to goodness, knowledge; and to knowledge, self-control; and to self-control, perseverance; and to perseverance, godliness; and to godliness, brotherly kindness; and to brotherly kindness, love. For if you possess these qualities in increasing measure, they will keep you from being ineffective and unproductive in your knowledge of our Lord Jesus Christ. But if anyone does not have them, he is nearsighted and blind, and has forgotten that he has been cleansed from his past sins (2 Peter 1:5-9).

Peter says, "For this very reason" (2 Peter 1:5). The reason is to participate in the divine nature and escape the corruption in the world. Peter said in verse 3 that God "has given us everything we need for life and godliness." If we have that, why do we need to "add" (v. 5)? God makes "additional" Christian graces, or attributes, available to us which we can add to our faith foundation. Things like the armor of God (Ephesians 6) are available to the believer, but we must make a decision to put that armor on. The fruit of the Spirit (Galatians 5) is available to us, but we must utilize the power that the indwelling Spirit brings to us to make them part of our spiritual make-up.

Peter uses the phrase "make every effort," or similar language, three times in critical passages. In 2 Peter 1:5-7 we find: "For this very reason, make every effort to add to your faith goodness." In verses 10, 11 we find: "Therefore, my brothers, be all the more eager to make your calling and election sure." In 2 Peter 3:14 we find: "So then, dear friends, since you are looking forward to this, make every effort to be found spotless, blameless and at peace with him."

When I look at the Christian graces, the first thing that impresses me is that God has granted them to us. They are gifts that He has made available to us, and we can appropriate them by an active faith, a faith made possible by God's righteousness (2 Peter 1:1). Notice: "For if you possess these qualities in increasing measure" (v. 8). All Christians have these qualities in some measure. What God wants is continual growth.

What does it mean to be "ineffective and unproductive" (2 Peter 1:8)? It means that these fruits are essential; first in our personal relationship with God and second in being used by God to bring others to Him. This is the heart of how God intended for the gospel to produce growth; not by experts, statistics, programs, and marketing strategies, but by

98

Christians demonstrating changed lives and attitudes. Peter says that the Christian who doesn't have these qualities "in increasing measure" (v. 8) has forgotten that he was purged. He has forgotten what that means. God has not saved us so that we can run around saying, "I'm saved, I'm saved," but so that we can exhibit regeneration and sanctification.

Therefore, my brothers, be all the more eager to make your calling and election sure. For if you do these things, you will never fall, and you will receive a rich welcome into the eternal kingdom of our Lord and Savior Jesus Christ (2 Peter 1:10, 11).

What is our "calling"? In 1 Corinthians 1:2 Paul says that those at Corinth who were "sanctified in Christ Jesus" were "called to be holy." In verse 9 he says that they were "called ... into fellowship with his Son Jesus Christ our Lord." Calling people to God through the gospel is the work of the Holy Spirit. Responding to the gospel is not simply an intellectual and rational response to the presentation of certain biblical facts or theological arguments. It is that, but it is much more than that. The Holy Spirit Himself seeks to convict the human conscience and decision-making process by speaking a vital message through the Scriptures.

In John 15:26, 27 Jesus says to the Twelve: "When the Counselor comes, whom I will send to you from the Father, the Spirit of truth who goes out from the Father, he will testify about me. And you also must testify, for you have been with me from the beginning." The "also" of this verse clearly distinguishes between the testimony of the disciples and the testimony of the Holy Spirit.

In John 16:7-11 He adds

> "But I tell you the truth: It is for your good that I am going away. Unless I go away, the Counselor will not come to you; but if I go, I will send him to you. When he comes, he will convict the world of guilt in regard to sin and righteousness and judgment: in regard to sin, because men do not believe in me; in regard to righteousness, because I am going to the Father, where you can see me no longer; and in regard to judgment, because the prince of this world now stands condemned."

From Acts 2:14-18,

> Then Peter stood up with the Eleven, raised his voice and addressed the crowd: "Fellow Jews and all of you who live in Jerusalem, let me explain this to you; listen carefully to what I say. These men are not drunk, as you suppose. It's only nine in the morning! No, this is what was spoken by the prophet Joel: 'In the last days, God says, I will pour out my Spirit on all people. Your sons and daughters will prophesy, your young men will see visions, your old men will dream dreams. Even on my servants, both men and women, I will pour out my Spirit in those days, and they will prophesy.' "

Election has to do with being chosen. (See chapter 1 on 1 Peter 1:1, 2 on the topic of election.) In Ephesians 1:4 Paul writes: He "chose us" in Christ, and in verse 11 he says, "[H]aving been predestined according to the plan of him who works out everything in conformity with the purpose of his will."

Peter says that the fruits we bear are not only the guarantee of our salvation, they bring assurance to us. In 1 Corinthians 3:5-15 Paul says

> What, after all, is Apollos? And what is Paul? Only servants, through whom you came to believe—as the Lord has assigned to each his task. I planted the seed, Apollos watered it, but God made it grow. So neither he who plants nor he who waters is anything, but only God, who makes things grow. The man who plants and the man who waters have one purpose, and each will be rewarded according to his own labor. For we are God's fellow workers; you are God's field, God's building. By the grace God has given me, I laid a foundation as an expert builder, and someone else is building on it. But each one should be careful how he builds. For no one can lay any foundation other than the one already laid, which is Jesus Christ. If any man builds on this foundation using gold, silver, costly stones, wood, hay or straw, his work will be shown for what it is, because the Day will bring it to light. It will be revealed with fire, and the fire will test the quality of each man's work. If what he has built survives, he will receive his reward. If it is burned up, he will suffer loss; he himself will be saved, but only as one escaping through the flames.

We can see the direct connection between what Peter means by doing these things in order to make our "calling and election sure" (2 Peter

1:10) and the guarantee that is ours through the indwelling Holy Spirit. From Ephesians 1:11-14: "In him we were also chosen, having been predestined according to the plan of him who works out everything in conformity with the purpose of his will, in order that we, who were the first to hope in Christ, might be for the praise of his glory. And you also were included in Christ when you heard the word of truth, the gospel of your salvation. Having believed, you were marked in him with a seal, the promised Holy Spirit, who is a deposit guaranteeing our inheritance until the redemption of those who are God's possession—to the praise of his glory." It is the Holy Spirit who creates the fruits both within and without, and it is the fruits that bring assurance.

So I will always remind you of these things, even though you know them and are firmly established in the truth you now have. I think it is right to refresh your memory as long as I live in the tent of this body, because I know that I will soon put it aside, as our Lord Jesus Christ has made clear to me. And I will make every effort to see that after my departure you will always be able to remember these things. We did not follow cleverly invented stories when we told you about the power and coming of our Lord Jesus Christ, but we were eyewitnesses of his majesty. For he received honor and glory from God the Father when the voice came to him from the Majestic Glory, saying, "This is my Son, whom I love; with him I am well pleased." We ourselves heard this voice that came from heaven when we were with him on the sacred mountain (2 Peter 1:12-18).

Peter knew that Christians would forget even some foundational aspects of our relationship with God. That is why it is so important for Christians to read their Bibles regularly and to listen to those who teach it.

Peter makes a strong argument for the necessity of accepting apostolic authority. That authority is based on those who saw the Christ in the flesh, heard Him speak, and witnessed His miracles, the crucifixion, and the resurrection. For Peter, there was a special closeness to the Christ because he witnessed the transfiguration—"when the voice came to him from the Majestic Glory, saying, 'This is my Son, whom I love; with him I am well pleased.' We ourselves heard this voice that came from heaven when we were with him on the sacred mountain" (2 Peter 1:17, 18). God makes it perfectly clear to Peter that he should listen to no voice, not even Moses or Elijah, but only to the voice of the Christ.

Peter says that there was nothing complicated about the gospel message he proclaimed. The preaching of the apostles was not based on myth, hyperbole, or exaggeration. It was based on what they saw and heard from the Christ Himself for three years. They *heard* the "Majestic" voice. Essentially, that message was: repent or perish.

Questions for 2 Peter 1:5-18

1. Peter uses the phrase "make every effort," or similar language, three times in critical passages. Does the idea of making every effort fly in the face of salvation by grace?

2. What does it mean to be ineffective and unfruitful?

3. Why is accepting "apostolic authority" so important?

4. Why does Peter feel the need to "remind" these Christians?

5. Peter says that we should make our calling and election sure. What is our "calling"? How are we "called"? How can we "make it sure"?

6. What does it mean to be "elected"?

7. List several things of which Peter "reminds" his readers.

And we have the word of the prophets made more certain, and you will do well to pay attention to it, as to a light shining in a dark place, until the day dawns and the morning star rises in your hearts. Above all, you must understand that no prophecy of Scripture came about by the prophet's own interpretation. For prophecy never had its origin in the will of man, but men spoke from God as they were carried along by the Holy Spirit (2 Peter 1:19-21).

The Old Testament prophecies of the coming of the Messiah have been verified by their fulfillment in Christ. The faith that lived in the prophets who spoke of things they little understood and knew they would never live to see fulfilled serves as an example for us. Their faith is a light to lead us to God. Believing and understanding their lives and their message will strengthen our faith and relationship with God.

Peter says that prophecy did not originate with the prophets; it originated with God. The prophets did not interpret their own prophecies—except as directed by God. All prophecy must be understood in the context of God's purposes. It is not given to us to interpret prophecy in any way that is inconsistent with God's eternal plan.

It is critical that we remember that what the prophets spoke was strictly confined to the words that God gave them. Isaiah, Moses, Jeremiah, Daniel, and Amos did not *decide* to be prophets. They were called by God, and they didn't have to stay up nights wondering what to say.

Questions for 2 Peter 1:19-21

1. Where did prophecy originate?

2. How did the writers of the Bible know what to write?

SECOND PETER

SECOND PETER
CHAPTER 2

But there were also false prophets among the people, just as there will be false teachers among you. They will secretly introduce destructive heresies, even denying the sovereign Lord who bought them—bringing swift destruction on themselves. Many will follow their shameful ways and will bring the way of truth into disrepute. In their greed these teachers will exploit you with stories they have made up. Their condemnation has long been hanging over them, and their destruction has not been sleeping (2 Peter 2:1-3).

Peter has already affirmed the credibility of the apostles in 2 Peter 1:16 when he says: "We did not follow cleverly invented stories when we told you about the power and coming of our Lord Jesus Christ, but we were eyewitnesses of his majesty." Peter says that there were false prophets under the old covenant, and there will be false prophets under the new covenant. False prophets posed a serious spiritual threat to the nation of Israel, and they pose a serious threat to every congregation of God's people.

Listen carefully to God's Word through Jeremiah in Jeremiah 14:14-16: "Then the LORD said to me, 'The prophets are prophesying lies in my name. I have not sent them or appointed them or spoken to them. They are prophesying to you false visions, divinations, idolatries and the delusions of their own minds. Therefore, this is what the LORD says about the prophets who are prophesying in my name: I did not send them, yet they are saying, "No sword or famine will touch this land." Those same prophets will perish by sword and famine. And the people they are prophesying to will be thrown out into the streets of Jerusalem because of the famine and sword. There will be no one to

But there were also false prophets among the people, just as there will be false teachers among you. They will secretly introduce destructive heresies, even denying the sovereign Lord who bought them—bringing swift destruction on themselves. Many will follow their shameful ways and will bring the way of truth into disrepute. In their greed these teachers will exploit you with stories they have made up. Their condemnation has long been hanging over them, and their destruction has not been sleeping (2 Peter 2:1-3).

Peter has already affirmed the credibility of the apostles in 2 Peter 1:16 when he says: "We did not follow cleverly invented stories when we told you about the power and coming of our Lord Jesus Christ, but we were eyewitnesses of his majesty." Peter says that there were false prophets under the old covenant, and there will be false prophets under the new covenant. False prophets posed a serious spiritual threat to the nation of Israel, and they pose a serious threat to every congregation of God's people.

Listen carefully to God's Word through Jeremiah in Jeremiah 14:14-16: "Then the LORD said to me, 'The prophets are prophesying lies in my name. I have not sent them or appointed them or spoken to them. They are prophesying to you false visions, divinations, idolatries and the delusions of their own minds. Therefore, this is what the LORD says about the prophets who are prophesying in my name: I did not send them, yet they are saying, "No sword or famine will touch this land." Those same prophets will perish by sword and famine. And the people they are prophesying to will be thrown out into the streets of Jerusalem because of the famine and sword. There will be no one to bury them or their wives, their sons or their daughters. I will pour out on them the calamity they deserve.'"

God says that everyone will suffer because of false prophets—including the prophets themselves. Jesus warned the disciples about false teachers in Matthew 7:15-20,

"Watch out for false prophets. They come to you in sheep's clothing, but inwardly they are ferocious wolves. By their fruit you will recognize them. Do people pick grapes from thornbushes, or figs from thistles? Likewise every good tree bears good fruit, but a bad tree bears bad fruit. A good tree cannot bear bad fruit, and a bad tree cannot bear good fruit. Every tree that does not bear good fruit is cut down and thrown into the fire. Thus, by their fruit you will recognize them."

Jesus says that false teachers do not come wearing a sign that says, "I am a false teacher." They come wearing the smiles and humble gestures of authorities with "special" knowledge, friends, and helpers. Jesus says that we need to judge them by their "fruit," not their appearance; and by their deeds, not their words. What kind of fruit does a false teacher bear? Often, if you listen closely, you will find that their message is about themselves—not the Christ. They speak more about the material aspects of the kingdom of God than the spiritual aspects.

Please do not overlook the fact that if false teachers didn't tell people what they wanted to hear, no one would follow them. They promise to solve all problems and provide the material blessings of wealth, health, and happiness—with a little eternal reward thrown in occasionally. Think about the book *The Prayer of Jabez*. What made it sell? It appealed to people's greed, but the only person who got rich off of it was the author.

False prophets create a dependency on themselves rather than on God. In Matthew 24:24 Jesus says: "For false Christs and false prophets will appear and perform great signs and miracles to deceive even the elect—if that were possible." Many false prophets claim great power to heal and to make our material dreams come true. Joseph Smith, Brigham Young, Sun Myung Moon, Oral Roberts, Benny Hinn, and the Bakkers—the list is endless. And people flock to their religions in droves because they would much rather believe a pleasant lie than an unpleasant truth.

Paul writes to the congregation at Corinth in 2 Corinthians 11:4: "For if someone comes to you and preaches a Jesus other than the Jesus we preached, or if you receive a different spirit from the one you received, or a different gospel from the one you accepted, you put up with it easily enough." Then note verse 13: "For such men are false apostles, deceitful workmen, masquerading as apostles of Christ."

Who is this "other Jesus" that Paul talks about? It is a Jesus who is Savior and not Lord. It is a Jesus who is "Lamb of God," but not "Lion of the tribe of Judah." It is a Jesus whose unconditional love prohibits Him from saying "No" to any request and who certainly would not think of sending anyone to hell. It is a Jesus who is something less than what the Messiah of God revealed Himself to be. Why did they "put up with it"? Because what they heard preached was more pleasant and easier than the gospel of cross bearing, self-sacrifice, service, and suffering.

Paul writes in 1 Timothy 1:3-7,

As I urged you when I went into Macedonia, stay there in Ephesus so that you may command certain men not to teach false doctrines any longer nor to devote themselves to myths and endless genealogies. These promote controversies rather than God's work—which is by faith. The goal of this command is love, which comes from a pure heart and a good conscience and a sincere faith. Some have wandered away from these and turned to meaningless talk. They want to be teachers of the law, but they do not know what they are talking about or what they so confidently affirm.

Again from 1 Timothy 6:3-5: "If anyone teaches false doctrines and does not agree to the sound instruction of our Lord Jesus Christ and to godly teaching, he is conceited and understands nothing. He has an unhealthy interest in controversies and quarrels about words that result in envy, strife, malicious talk, evil suspicions and constant friction between men of corrupt mind, who have been robbed of the truth and who think that godliness is a means to financial gain."

"Myths and endless genealogies" are the kinds of highly figurative and vague issues and doctrines that allow for speculation. False teachers seize upon those areas of Scripture, like spiritual gifts and end of times teaching, where they can claim to have answers to difficult and obscure doctrines and attract followers who enjoy imaginative speculations and subjective interpretations on topics that have nothing to do with either salvation or holiness. The strife, malicious talk, constant friction, and controversy that necessarily follow as a result of these teachings are used by Satan to distract Christians from their focus on the cross and proclaiming the gospel. They place the focus on the one who is claiming to have special knowledge rather than on the Christ. Somewhere behind most false teaching is a power or monetary motive.

It is critical to note that there is such a thing as "sound doctrine." That sound doctrine is centered in and focused on the advent, ministry, teaching, lifestyle, death, burial, and resurrection of the Christ.

Peter lists the qualities of false teachers:

1. They secretly introduce "destructive heresies" (2 Peter 2:1).

2. They deny the sonship (divinity) of Jesus (v.1).

3. They are motivated by "greed" (v. 3).

4. They "despise authority"—other than their own, of course (v. 10).

5. They are "bold and arrogant" (v. 10).
6. They are shamelessly immoral (vv. 13, 14).
7. They are governed by materialistic motivations (vv. 3, 14).
8. They make empty promises (v. 18) like health, wealth, happiness, healing, instant success and guaranteed salvation.
9. They promise "freedom" (v. 19), but they enslave their followers to themselves. (What many restoration congregation members may remember as the Boston Movement, later called the United Churches of Christ, is a prime and painful example of this.)
10. False teachers prey on the simple-minded, the hurting, the biblically uninformed, and those who are new to Christianity.

Is there a difference between an honest misunderstanding of Scripture and a false teacher? Yes, I believe there is, but unfortunately, both can have the same effect. The difference is that a humble teacher always tries to differentiate between his personal understanding of a difficult passage and an inspired understanding of it. He also does not *insist* that people accept his interpretation of difficult passages, and a false teacher does.

Do we still have false teachers? With three hundred brands of Christianity, each preaching its personal agenda and peculiar doctrines which often openly deny the inspiration of the Bible and have little to do with the central truths of Scripture, of course we do! We don't have much trouble identifying religious movements like the New Age Movement, the Church of Christ Scientist, Catholics, Episcopalians, and the Mormons as teaching false doctrine, but it gets a little more difficult when it comes to Methodists, Baptists, Christian Churches, and the Disciples. How do we recognize them? Jesus said, "by their fruit" (Matthew 7:20).

Who makes false prophets successful? People do! As long as there are people who would rather hear a pleasant or flattering lie than an unpleasant and unflattering truth, we will find those who will tell us what we wish to hear. As long as there are people who willfully remain ignorant of the biblical message and are too lazy to challenge and investigate what they are being taught, we will have false teachers. We create false prophets by allowing ourselves to be lulled by what is pleasant, soothing, and satisfying. Not only do we *allow* it, we *insist* upon it and dismiss from our hearing those who teach us the hard sayings of Scripture.

Questions for 2 Peter 2:1-3

1. Who is a false teacher or false prophet? How do we recognize them?
2. What are the signs of a false teacher?
3. What kinds of promises do false teachers make?
4. Is there a difference between an honest misunderstanding of Scripture and a false teacher?
5. What makes false teachers successful?
6. Where do most false teachers operate?
7. What is the best defense against false teachers?
8. Are elders and evangelists exempt from being false teachers?

For if God did not spare angels when they sinned, but sent them to hell, putting them into gloomy dungeons to be held for judgment; if he did not spare the ancient world when he brought the flood on its ungodly people, but protected Noah, a preacher of righteousness, and seven others; if he condemned the cities of Sodom and Gomorrah by burning them to ashes, and made them an example of what is going to happen to the ungodly; and if he rescued Lot, a righteous man, who was distressed by the filthy lives of lawless men (for that righteous man, living among them day after day, was tormented in his righteous soul by the lawless deeds he saw and heard)—if this is so, then the Lord knows how to rescue godly men from trials and to hold the unrighteous for the day of judgment, while continuing their punishment. This is especially true of those who follow the corrupt desire of the sinful nature and despise authority. Bold and arrogant, these men are not afraid to slander celestial beings; yet even angels, although they are stronger and more powerful, do not bring slanderous accusations against such beings in the presence of the Lord. But these men blaspheme in matters they do not understand. They are like brute beasts, creatures of instinct, born only to be caught and destroyed, and like beasts they too will perish (2 Peter 2:4-12).

This passage is almost identical to Jude. Peter says that God not only has the power to punish the disobedient, but He has demonstrated that He has the will to do it. "They will be paid back with harm for the harm they have done" (2 Peter 2:13). But it is comforting to know that God also has the desire, the power, and the will to rescue the righteous from trials.

Peter is not embarrassed to speak clearly and vividly of hell. It is important that those who faithfully follow God's Word present a balanced view of the glories of heaven and the terrors of hell. The gospel is "good news," but an important part of that good news is the concept of salvation. But salvation has no meaning apart from what we are being saved *from*—hell—and what we are being saved to—heaven. The desire to go to heaven is multiplied by the fear of going to hell.

It is much easier to get so caught up in secondary issues, like political corruption, world hunger and poverty, abortion, homosexuality, pornography, civil rights, and sex education that we forget that they are merely symptoms of a far deeper problem—sin and being lost. Our mission as the children of God is primarily to preach the gospel—until people come into a relationship with God through the cross, no lasting or eternal changes have been made.

Jesus said that He came into the world for two purposes—to show us the Father and to seek and save the lost (John 14:7-10; Luke 19:10). All other considerations were secondary to that. Jesus could have clothed, fed, built a house for, and healed everybody in the entire world, but that was not His purpose—and it is not ours. His focus must be our focus. If it is not, we cannot claim to be His disciples. Mark 16:15, 16 contains what we call "the Great Commission": "He said to them, 'Go into all the world and preach the good news to all creation. Whoever believes and is baptized will be saved, but whoever does not believe will be condemned.' "

In Matthew 10:28 Jesus says to His disciples: "Do not be afraid of those who kill the body but cannot kill the soul. Rather, be afraid of the One who can destroy both soul and body in hell." In Mark 9:48 Jesus describes hell as a place where "their worm does not die, and the fire is not quenched."

Restoration congregations have the reputation of being an issue-conscious, sometimes belligerent and somewhat contentious religious movement. We can skillfully discuss various areas of theology, but we are not noted for our evangelistic zeal. Many of the issues that are attracting our attention and to which we are devoting much of our energy have little to do with either personal holiness, the fruit of the

Spirit, or taking the gospel to the lost. But it is easy to come away from one of these discussions thinking ourselves very spiritual because we believe "right things" about the doctrines of Scripture.

In 2 Peter 2:11-22 Peter continues to describe false teachers, indicating how arrogant they are in pushing their opinions on others about matters totally beyond their scope of understanding, and what a horrible end awaits them.

They will be paid back with harm for the harm they have done. Their idea of pleasure is to carouse in broad daylight. They are blots and blemishes, reveling in their pleasures while they feast with you. With eyes full of adultery, they never stop sinning; they seduce the unstable; they are experts in greed—an accursed brood! They have left the straight way and wandered off to follow the way of Balaam son of Beor, who loved the wages of wickedness. But he was rebuked for his wrongdoing by a donkey—a beast without speech—who spoke with a man's voice and restrained the prophet's madness. These men are springs without water and mists driven by a storm. Blackest darkness is reserved for them. For they mouth empty, boastful words and, by appealing to the lustful desires of sinful human nature, they entice people who are just escaping from those who live in error. They promise them freedom, while they themselves are slaves of depravity—for a man is a slave to whatever has mastered him. If they have escaped the corruption of the world by knowing our Lord and Savior Jesus Christ and are again entangled in it and overcome, they are worse off at the end than they were at the beginning. It would have been better for them not to have known the way of righteousness, than to have known it and then to turn their backs on the sacred command that was passed on to them. Of them the proverbs are true: "A dog returns to its vomit," and, "A sow that is washed goes back to her wallowing in the mud" (2 Peter 2:13-22).

God will hold these men accountable for the harm they have caused. After reading the description Peter gives of these false teachers, it comes as somewhat of a shock to hear him suggest that they are working from inside the community of faith and participating in congregational affairs. However, it is important to remember that the greatest harm that has come to the church has always come from inside. When Paul calls for the elders of the congregation in Ephesus to come to Miletus to visit him, he warns them that the greatest threat facing the congregation will come from among the elders themselves (see Acts 20:30). Peter refers to "the straight way" (2 Peter 2:15), and we would all do well to seek that way.

Peter warns that the promises false teachers make are empty. They promise freedom, health, wealth, peace, and prosperity; but they cannot deliver what they have promised. Unfortunately, people continue to believe and support preachers who tell them what they want to hear. False teachers prey on the simple-minded, the hurting, the biblically uninformed, and those who are new to Christianity. False teachers are the victims of their own deception. They believe that they are in control, failing to realize that they are slaves to their own passions and to the prince of darkness. There is a special dispensation of the wrath of God reserved for the false teacher. In fact, Peter says that they would have been better off to have never come in contact with the gospel than to have received it and then distorted it to their own selfish ends in order to deceive others (2 Peter 2:20, 21).

Questions for 2 Peter 2:4-22

1. What will happen to all false teachers in the end?

2. Why is it important that those who faithfully follow God's Word present a *balanced* view of the glories of heaven and the terrors of hell?

3. Do you believe that the desire to go to heaven is multiplied by the fear of going to hell?

4. What are the two purposes for which Jesus said He came into the world?

5. Restoration congregations are not noted for our evangelistic zeal. Why?

6. Why may we be surprised to hear that these false teachers are working from the "inside"? What does that mean?

7. Who are the favorite victims of false teachers?

8. What is the "straight way"?

SECOND PETER

SECOND PETER
CHAPTER 3

Dear friends, this is now my second letter to you. I have written both of them as reminders to stimulate you to wholesome thinking. I want you to recall the words spoken in the past by the holy prophets and the command given by our Lord and Savior through your apostles (2 Peter 3:1, 2).

Peter says that the reason he is writing is to stir them up to "wholesome thinking." The word "wholesome" suggests health, completeness, and soundness. It is healthy thinking that takes in the whole picture of the meaning of creation, revelation, life, death, and resurrection.

1. It is thinking that takes in the scope of God's revelation and activity.
2. It is thinking that sees life through the lens of the complete revelation of God in Scripture and understands that life has a single purpose—to know God.
3. Wholesome thinking is thinking that places all material activity and human aspiration in the light of "the day of the Lord" (2 Peter 3:10).
4. The second coming of the Christ and the judgment of God cause Christians to judge the value and importance of every event and circumstance from a totally different perspective.

Wholesome thinking is thinking that is dominated by the "mind of Christ." Philippians 2:1-8 says

"If you have any encouragement from being united with Christ, if any comfort from his love, if any fellowship with the Spirit, if any tenderness and compassion, then make my joy complete by being like-minded, having the same love, being one in spirit and purpose. Do nothing out of selfish ambition or vain conceit, but in humility consider others better than yourselves. Each of you should look not only to your own interests, but also to the interests of others. Your attitude should be the same as that of Christ Jesus: Who, being in very nature God, did not consider equality with God something to be grasped, but made himself nothing, taking the very nature of a servant, being made in human likeness. And being found in appearance as a man, he humbled himself and became obedient to death—even death on a cross!

Paul urges the Christians at Philippi to be "like-minded" and to be "one in spirit and purpose" (Philippians 2:2). Given the natural propensity of humans to be self-centered and disagreeable, how is that possible? Wholesome thinking means to have the mind of Christ. If all of us have His attitude of making Himself "nothing" (v. 7), then unity, harmony, and peace are not only possible—they are essential.

Now listen to what Paul says to the Corinthian congregation in 1 Corinthians 2:10-16:

The Spirit searches all things, even the deep things of God. For who among men knows the thoughts of a man except the man's spirit within him? In the same way no one knows the thoughts of God except the Spirit of God. We have not received the spirit of the world but the Spirit who is from God, that we may understand what God has freely given us. This is what we speak, not in words taught us by human wisdom but in words taught by the Spirit, expressing spiritual truths in spiritual words. The man without the Spirit does not accept the things that come from the Spirit of God, for they are foolishness to him, and he cannot understand them, because they are spiritually discerned. The spiritual man makes judgments about all things, but he himself is not subject to any man's judgment: "For who has known the mind of the Lord that he may instruct him?" But we have the mind of Christ.

Paul says that all Christians have received the Holy Spirit and that one of the things the Spirit does is to help us to understand what God has given us. That means that if we are listening to the Spirit, we will have a common understanding of God's revelation; because the Spirit will not teach one person one thing and another person something different. Paul concludes 1 Corinthians 2:16 by affirming that every child of God can have the "mind of Christ."

In Romans 12:1, 2, Paul gives us deeper insight into the source of wholesome thinking when he says: "Therefore, I urge you, brothers, in view of God's mercy, to offer your bodies as living sacrifices, holy and pleasing to God—this is your spiritual act of worship. Do not conform any longer to the pattern of this world, but be transformed by the renewing of your mind. Then you will be able to test and approve what God's will is—his good, pleasing and perfect will."

The offering of our bodies as living sacrifices has to do with our determination to not be controlled by fleshly desires. That offering is a spiritual sacrifice—as opposed to a physical or material one. That means that it is generated by the Holy Spirit. To "conform" to the pattern of the world means to accept social values rather than Christian values. It means to think in material terms rather than spiritual ones.

Paul says that we should be transformed and that transformation is the result of a renewed mind (Romans 12:2). How do we get renewed minds? Obviously, we do not have the power to do that on our own; it is something that we allow God to do in us. How does that happen? What role do we play? I think the answers to those questions are found in Romans 8:5-9, 12-14 where Paul says

> Those who live according to the sinful nature have their minds set on what that nature desires; but those who live in accordance with the Spirit have their minds set on what the Spirit desires. The mind of sinful man is death, but the mind controlled by the Spirit is life and peace; the sinful mind is hostile to God. It does not submit to God's law, nor can it do so. Those controlled by the sinful nature cannot please God. You, however, are controlled not by the sinful nature but by the Spirit, if the Spirit of God lives in you. And if anyone does not have the Spirit of Christ, he does not belong to Christ. ...Therefore, brothers, we have an obligation—but it is not to the sinful nature, to live according to it. For if you live according to the sinful nature, you will die; but if by the Spirit you put to death the misdeeds of the body, you will live, because those who are led by the Spirit of God are sons of God.

A renewed mind is a mind that is controlled by the Holy Spirit. It is a mind that sees everything in life from a spiritual perspective. It is a mind that has overcome the sinful nature—the force within us that makes us want to sin. It is a mind that looks for and sees God's purpose in every event and circumstance in life. It is a mind that sees everything through the eyes of faith.

First of all, you must understand that in the last days scoffers will come, scoffing and following their own evil desires. They will say, "Where is this 'coming' he promised? Ever since our fathers died, everything goes on as it has since the beginning of creation." But they deliberately forget that long ago by God's word the heavens existed and the earth was formed out of water and by water. By these waters also the world of that time was deluged and destroyed. By the same word the present heavens and earth are reserved for fire, being kept for the day of judgment and destruction of ungodly men. But do not forget this one thing, dear friends: With the Lord a day is like a thousand years, and a thousand years are like a day. The Lord is not slow in keeping his promise, as some understand slowness. He is patient with you, not wanting anyone to perish, but everyone to come to repentance (2 Peter 3:3-9).

Peter says that wholesome thinking recognizes that people will try to shake the faith of God's people by pointing out discrepancies in God's revelation. Why would they do that? Why would anyone care if folks believed in God and in His revelation? The faith of believers is seen as a condemnation to the unbelief of those who know them. The firm faith of believers, along with their lifestyle and attitudes that allow them to experience all of the circumstances of life—the good and the bad and especially the negative ones—and live lives of peace, joy, and contentment, is a faith that is a *choice* and is available to everyone.

Peter says that those who accuse God of not keeping His promises "deliberately forget" the facts of the past (2 Peter 3:5). Those who choose to live their lives as they please, without having to answer to God for their actions, have to find a way to justify their lifestyles and actions. They do that by willfully choosing to ignore any evidence that would lead to a different conclusion.

This principle is applicable to many areas of revelation. People have always tried to find a "loophole" in revelation in order to justify their determination to follow their own lusts. In Peter's day they discredited the idea of the resurrection and the second coming of Jesus. They do the same thing today so they can live as they want. They can justify greed, drunkenness, drug abuse, deceit, selfishness, homosexuality, divorce, abortion, premarital sex, and pornography.

Peter responds to their arguments against the second coming by reminding them of some facts about God. God has no sense of time (2 Peter 3:8, 9). God doesn't want anyone to be condemned; He gives them time and opportunity to repent.

Questions for 2 Peter 3:1-9

1. List four things that constitute "wholesome thinking".

2. In Romans 12, what does it mean to "conform ... to the pattern of this world"?

3. What role does the Holy Spirit play in helping us with "wholesome thinking"?

4. Do you think it is possible to be "like-minded" and to be "one in spirit and purpose" (Philippians 2:2)?

5. How do we get renewed minds?

6. To "conform" to the "pattern of this world" means to accept social values rather than Christian values (Romans 12:2). Do you believe that you are ever guilty of this? Can you think of a specific instance? When and how did you stop? How has your life changed?

7. Why would anyone care if someone else believed in God and in His revelation?

8. Why do people "deliberately forget" the things—like the flood—that God has done in the past (2 Peter 3:5, 6)?

9. What is God's concept of time? Why is that important?

But the day of the Lord will come like a thief. The heavens will disappear with a roar; the elements will be destroyed by fire, and the earth and everything in it will be laid bare. Since everything will be destroyed in this way, what kind of people ought you to be? You ought to live holy and godly lives as you look forward to the day of God and speed its coming. That day will bring about the destruction of the heavens by fire, and the elements will melt in the heat. But in keeping with his promise we are looking forward to a new heaven and a new earth, the home of righteousness (2 Peter 3:10-13).

Peter says Jesus is going to come back, and when He does we will have no warning. There will be no chance to say, "Wait, I want to change my life!" The second coming will result in the destruction of the universe.

Peter says that the imminent return of the Christ and the destruction of the universe ought to produce a dramatic change in our priorities, values, thoughts, and lifestyle. Peter asks, in view of these facts, how should we then live? He answers his own question by saying, "You ought to live holy and godly lives as you look forward to the day of God and speed its coming" (2 Peter 3:11, 12).

What is a "holy and godly" life? Holiness is associated with sanctification—total devotion, having a single focus of seeking after God with all our hearts. Holiness is having the mind of Christ, which means that we see people and this world as He saw it. It means valuing what He valued, loving what He loved, and doing the will of the Father.

Think about the words to these hymns we sing:

> More holiness give me; more strivings within. More patience in suffering; more sorrow for sin. More faith in my Savior; more sense of His care. More joy in His service; more purpose in prayer.
> —Philip P. Bliss, 1873

> Take time to be holy; speak oft with thy Lord. Abide in Him always, and feed on His word. Make friends of God's children; help those who are weak. Forgetting in nothing His blessing to seek.

> Take time to be holy; the world rushes on. Spend much time in secret, with Jesus alone. By looking to Jesus, like Him thou shalt be. Thy friends in thy conduct, His likeness shall see.

> Take time to be holy; be calm in thy soul. Each thought and each motive beneath His control. Thus led by His Spirit to fountains of love; Thou soon shall be fitted for service above."
> —George Stebbins, 1890

A holy and godly life is a life that is filled with pursuing things that have eternal consequences. We are prone to think that the goal of holiness is to empty ourselves of bad actions and bad thoughts. The result of a negative approach to holiness and Christianity is that often we end up doing and thinking nothing. C.S. Lewis in his marvelous work, *The Screwtape Letters*, has something important to say about "nothing." For those of you who have never had the pleasure of reading this incredibly insightful work about how Satan works in our lives, let me simply say that you really need to. I encourage you to especially read letter number 12.

Peter insists that Christians ought to be looking forward to that day (2 Peter 3:12). What might keep us from that? The more we have here, the less desire we have to leave it. The more we love the things of the world, the less desire we have to leave them. The more focused we are on the "seen," the material, the less focused we are on the eternal.

Peter talks about a "new heaven and a new earth" (2 Peter 3:13). What does that mean to you? How do you visualize this new heaven and earth? Read these three passages carefully and allow your imagination to create a visual image of these scenes:

Revelation 7:9-17:

After this I looked and there before me was a great multitude that no one could count, from every nation, tribe, people and language, standing before the throne and in front of the Lamb. They were wearing white robes and were holding palm branches in their hands. And they cried out in a loud voice: "Salvation belongs to our God, who sits on the throne, and to the Lamb." All the angels were standing around the throne and around the elders and the four living creatures. They fell down on their faces before the throne and worshiped God, saying: "Amen! Praise and glory and wisdom and thanks and honor and power and strength be to our God for ever and ever. Amen!" Then one of the elders asked me, "These in white robes—who are they, and where did they come from?" I answered, "Sir, you know." And he said, "These are they who have come out of the great tribulation; they have washed their robes and made them white in the blood of the Lamb. Therefore, they are before the throne of God and serve him day and night in his temple; and he who sits on the throne will spread his tent over them. Never again will they hunger; never again will they thirst. The sun will not beat upon them, nor any scorching heat. For the Lamb at the center of the throne will be their shepherd; he will lead them to springs of living water. And God will wipe away every tear from their eyes."

Revelation 20:11-15:

Then I saw a great white throne and him who was seated on it. Earth and sky fled from his presence, and there was no place for them. And I saw the dead, great and small, standing before the throne, and books were opened. Another book was opened, which is the book of life. The dead were judged according to what they had done as recorded in the books. The sea gave up the dead that were in it, and death and Hades gave up the dead that were in them, and each person was judged according to what he had done. Then death and Hades were thrown into the lake of fire. The lake of fire is the second death. If anyone's name was not found written in the book of life, he was thrown into the lake of fire.

Revelation 21:1-8:

Then I saw a new heaven and a new earth, for the first heaven and the first earth had passed away, and there was no longer any sea. I saw the Holy City, the new Jerusalem, coming down out of heaven from God, prepared as a bride beautifully dressed for her husband. And I heard a loud voice from the throne saying, "Now the dwelling of God is with men, and he will live with them. They will be his people, and God himself will be with them and be their God. He will wipe every tear from their eyes. There will be no more death or mourning or crying or pain, for the old order of things has passed away." He who was seated on the throne said, "I am making everything new!" Then he said, "Write this down, for these words are trustworthy and true." He said to me: "It is done. I am the Alpha and the Omega, the Beginning and the End. To him who is thirsty I will give to drink without cost from the spring of the water of life. He who overcomes will inherit all this, and I will be his God and he will be my son. But the cowardly, the unbelieving, the vile, the murderers, the sexually immoral, those who practice magic arts, the idolaters and all liars—their place will be in the fiery lake of burning sulfur. This is the second death.'

These verses contain visions of eternity that would be well worth believing even if they weren't true; but believing with all our hearts that they are true and that we can actually be there in person makes them all the more precious.

Questions for 2 Peter 3:10-13

1. When Jesus comes back, how much time will people have to repent?
2. In view of the imminent second coming of Jesus, how should we be living? Are you living that way?
3. What might keep us from looking forward to the coming of Christ?
4. How would you describe a "holy and godly" life (2 Peter 3:11)?
5. How does reading about the events described in the Revelation passages included in this chapter affect you? What do you find most interesting? What do you find most frightening? What do you find most exciting?
6. What do you think this "new heaven" and "new earth" are going to look like (2 Peter 3:13)?

So then, dear friends, since you are looking forward to this, make every effort to be found spotless, blameless and at peace with him. Bear in mind that our Lord's patience means salvation, just as our dear brother Paul also wrote you with the wisdom that God gave him. He writes the same way in all his letters, speaking in them of these matters. His letters contain some things that are hard to understand, which ignorant and unstable people distort, as they do the other Scriptures, to their own destruction (2 Peter 3:14-16).

"So then." Peter presumes upon our agreement with what he has been saying. Because we have accepted as truth the promise of our resurrection, the destruction of the material world, and the subsequent judgment of God, we should "make every effort" (2 Peter 3:14). Why? Being a Christian is tough. The gate is narrow, and the way is straight. If it were easy, everybody would be a Christian.

Our effort is directed toward being "spotless, blameless and at peace" with God (2 Peter 3:14). How do we do that? Perhaps the obvious answer would be through diligence in assembling with God's people; diligence in singing hymns of praise; with prayers of thanksgiving, hope, and faith; and studying and meditating on God's Word—and that is certainly true. I would challenge all of us to consider that how we make practical application of what the Holy Spirit convicts us of through the Scriptures may play the most vital role in our becoming "spotless, blameless, and at peace with Him" (v. 14).

Ephesians 4:22-32:

You were taught, with regard to your former way of life, to put off your old self, which is being corrupted by its deceitful desires; to be made new in the attitude of your minds; and to put on the new self, created to be like God in true righteousness and holiness. Therefore each of you must put off falsehood and speak truthfully to his neighbor, for we are all members of one body. "In your anger do not sin": Do not let the sun go down while you are still angry, and do not give the devil a foothold. He who has been stealing must steal no longer, but must work, doing something useful with his own hands, that he may have something to share with those in need. Do not let any unwholesome talk come out of your mouths, but only what is helpful for building others up according to their needs, that it may benefit those who listen. And do not grieve the Holy Spirit of God, with whom you were sealed for the day of redemption. Get rid of all bitterness, rage and anger, brawling and slander, along with every form of malice. Be kind and compassionate to one another, forgiving each other, just as in Christ God forgave you.

It is because God wants more people to have the opportunity to be saved that He does not destroy the world now. He refers to the writings of Paul on this same topic. And he says that Paul has written some things that are hard to understand, which "ignorant ... people distort" (2 Peter 3:16). Amen!

Questions for 2 Peter 3:14-16

1. Does Peter's admonition to "make every effort" (2 Peter 3:14) conflict with salvation by grace?
2. Being a Christian is tough. In what specific ways is your Christian life sometimes difficult?
3. How can we be "spotless, blameless and at peace" with God (2 Peter 3:14)?
4. What does Ephesians 4 teach us about handling anger?

Therefore, dear friends, since you already know this, be on your guard so that you may not be carried away by the error of lawless men and

fall from your secure position. But grow in the grace and knowledge of our Lord and Savior Jesus Christ. To him be glory both now and forever! Amen (2 Peter 3:17, 18).

Peter essentially says, "I know that you already know this, but I needed to remind you—because it is so easy to forget, and Satan is so clever. His servants can make this world look so good, and what they promise is so enticing because it appeals to the sinful nature; and we want to believe it so badly."

What is our "secure position" (2 Peter 3:17)? If it is secure, how can we fall from it? God's promises are secure—not our reception of them. Those promises are

1. forgiveness through the cross

2. sonship through the new birth

3. knowing Him through the Holy Spirit

4. peace through trust

5. everlasting life because He has promised it

6. security is based on salvation by grace

It is our failure to respond appropriately to God's promises that can cause us to fall. We are to "grow in the grace and knowledge of our Lord and Savior Jesus Christ" (2 Peter 3:18). How do we grow in grace? First, I believe that the more we are aware of and acknowledge the grace of God in our lives, the more convicted we will be of our unworthiness. It is the feeling of unworthiness that creates humility, and humility leads to a greater appreciation for God's grace. Second, the more aware we are of our need for grace, the more willing we will be to extend it to others. Both of those things will make us more like Jesus.

What does it mean to grow in the knowledge of Jesus? I believe it has two facets. First, it means to grow in the factual knowledge of who He is. The Hebrew writer makes a valiant attempt to do this, by explaining that He is the "firstborn" of all creation, that He played a critical role in creation, that He is higher than the angels and greater than Abraham and even Melchizedek. He is our high priest. Second, it has to do with knowing Him in the sense of experience. Remember what Jesus said in John 17:3: "Now this is eternal life: that they may know you, the only true God, and Jesus Christ, whom you have sent." He equates salvation itself with knowing God. That is an idea worth reaching for.

Remember also that Jesus said that He came to "show us the Father."

He tells Thomas in John 14:7: "If you really knew me, you would know my Father as well. From now on, you do know him and have seen him." When Philip says, "Lord, show us the Father and that will be enough for us," Jesus says to him: "Don't you know me, Philip, even after I have been among you such a long time? Anyone who has seen me has seen the Father. How can you say, 'Show us the Father'?" (vv. 8, 9).

Knowing God factually is much easier than knowing Him experientially. But we can never know Him experientially until we know Him factually. The Scriptures reveal Him to us factually. The entire Bible is God saying to us: "This is who I am." But the Bible also reveals Him to us experientially by revealing His personality. Just as God is never content in where we are in our relationship with Him, so we must never be content in our relationship with God. Every step we take in His direction is simply a place from which to leap to a new level of spiritual maturity.

Questions for 2 Peter 3:17, 18

1. What is our "secure position" (2 Peter 3:17)? If it is secure, how can we fall from it?
2. How do we grow in the grace of Jesus?
3. How do we grow in the knowledge of Jesus?
4. What is the difference between knowing Jesus intellectually and factually and knowing Him experientially?
5. In what ways can we gain spiritual maturity?

NOTES ON
CALVIN AND ELECTION

John Calvin borrowed extensively from the theology and teachings of Martin Luther. The following is a list of the major tenets of his theology:

1. He believed in the inerrancy of Scripture.
2. He derived from it an organized religious system that was logical, efficient, and absolute. He used the Bible like a sledgehammer.
3. He believed that God is absolute; therefore God's decrees are absolute. There is no "give" in them and no "gray" areas.
4. Man's salvation is dependent on God's decrees and grace.
5. Human works and actions have no value in salvation.
6. God has completely predestined every act of each man's life.
7. God's only purpose in creation is His own glory.
8. Man is damned by God's ordinances and by his own inherited sin.
9. Damnation for some people is just as certain as election for others = predestination.

Calvin had no notion of God as loving, compassionate, forgiving, or patient, as we use those terms. He was a God of terror—whimsical, arbitrary, and not possessing a sense of justice or mercy as we understand that. Calvin did not distinguish between the Old Testament and the New Testament. Incidentally, neither did Luther or Zwingli. He did differentiate between the Levitical law and the Law of Moses, the Ten Commandments, but not between the Ten Commandments and the teachings of Jesus.

Calvin understood grace in a very restricted sense. As originally created, man was good and capable of obedience. When he fell, he lost both his goodness and the power to be good. The foundation for his concept of saving grace was his belief that man is born totally depraved, absolutely lost, and without moral freedom (that is, the ability to choose between good and evil) Calvin believed that all of mankind's choices are predetermined and that striving for godliness is useless.

Calvin said that man's highest knowledge is of God and himself. We can only know God through Scripture and the power of the indwelling Holy Spirit. Salvation is accomplished by the direct operation of the Holy Spirit who works at His own pleasure. Man can do nothing to encourage or discourage the work of the Holy Spirit.

Calvin said that man cannot be justified by good works. But he also said that we cannot be justified without them. He said that good works are proof of election, not the cause of election. A man is saved to do good works and produce Christian character, not by good works.

Calvin reasoned that because salvation is solely by grace, it must be by predestination. His logic is correct. If a person can do absolutely nothing to be saved, then all responsibility for salvation rests with God. One of the fallacies in Calvin's logic was that if anyone is lost, it has to be God's fault because they could do nothing to save themselves anyway.

A divine mandate once uttered cannot be revoked. God cannot change His mind. When Calvin read Psalm 139:21: "Do I not hate those who hate you," he said that we must hate all of God's enemies even though we should love our own. If God's will involves the destruction of evil, the evildoer is included. Tolerance toward evil people was a wicked doctrine because it demanded compromise with the devil. Calvin believed in "closed communion" and enforced it.

On paper Calvin seems harsh, unyielding, and opposed to the spirit of Christ. Fortunately, in actual practice, Calvinists were much better than their creed.

Calvin believed strongly in a church-state government, and that the church should take precedence over the state. He promoted an ecclesiastical hierarchy, a synod of elders that had absolute control over all church bodies. They combined political, police, and ecclesiastic power. (He instituted this because it was the pattern established by God in the nation of Israel.) Persons who were caught in sins were severely punished by church leaders. Everybody was closely watched to insure compliance. Even death by execution was part of Calvin's order, and many were killed by well-meaning churchmen—as in the Salem witch trials.

Simplicity in worship was stressed to a fanatical degree. It was a reaction to the extravagant, ritualistic ornateness and ceremony of Catholicism. Calvin would judge us harshly today for padded pews, air-conditioning, colored glass, athletic considerations, etc.

Calvin is largely responsible for the predominant role that singing was to play in the Protestant church, but he was dramatically opposed to the use of instrumental music.